100 LITERACY ASSESSMENT LESSONS

TERMS AND CONDITIONS

IMPORTANT – PERMITTED USE AND WARNINGS – READ CAREFULLY BEFORE USING

Licence

YEAR 4
Scottish Primary 5

Minimum specification:
- PC or Mac with a CD-ROM drive and 512 Mb RAM (recommended)
- Windows 98SE or above/Mac OS X.4 or above
- Recommended minimum processor speed: 1 GHz

For all technical support queries, please phone Scholastic Customer Services on 0845 603 9091.

Sylvia Clements

CREDITS

Author
Sylvia Clements

Development Editors
Kate Pedlar &
Niamh O'Carroll

Editor
Liz Dalby

Project Editor
Fabia Lewis

Series Designers
Melissa Leeke &
Joy Monkhouse

Designers
Quadrum Ltd &
Sonja Bagley

Illustrations
Bill Houston/Bill Houston
Creative Limited (unless
otherwise credited)

CD-ROM development
CD-ROM developed in
association with Vivid
Interactive

ACKNOWLEDGEMENTS

The publishers gratefully acknowledge permission to reproduce the following copyright material: **Moira Andrew** for 'Sea Seasons' from *Curriculum Bank: Poetry* by Moira Andrew © 1998, Moira Andrew (1998, Scholastic), 'Greengrocer' and 'Deserted Greenhouse' by Moira Andrew from *Scholastic Poetry Workshop Anthology* edited by David Orme © 1997, Moira Andrew (1997, Scholastic) and for 'Images of the Moon' adapted from an original idea by Moira Andrew. **Maggie Beard** for extracts from *Writing Guides: Activities for writing Fantasy* by Maggie Lovatt © 2001, Maggie Beard (2001, Scholastic). **David Higham Associates** for 'Cats' from *Blackbird has spoken: Selected Poems for Children* by Eleanor Farjeon © 1957, Eleanor Farjeon (1999, Macmillan); an extract from *Fantastic Mr Fox* by Roald Dahl ©1968, Roald Dahl (1968, Allen & Unwin) adapted by Sylvia Clements; extracts from *The Worry Website* by Jacqueline Wilson © 2002, Jacqueline Wilson (2002, Doubleday) adapted by Sylvia Clements; an extract from *Red Eyes at Night* by Michael Morpurgo © 1998, Michael Morpurgo (1998, Hodder) and an extract from *Loudmouth Louis* by Anne Fine © 1998, Anne Fine (1998, Puffin). **Faber and Faber** for 'Macavity –The Mystery Cat' from *Old Possum's Book of Practical Cats* by TS Eliot © 1974, TS Eliot (1974, Faber and Faber). **Floris Books** for an extract from *Bullies at School* by Theresa Breslin © 1993, Theresa Breslin (1993, Blackie). **John Foster** for 'What is slippery?', 'The Show Monster', 'January' and 'Hard Winters' from *Making Waves* by John Foster © 1997, John Foster (1997, Oxford University Press); 'Spring Snow' from *Climb aboard the poetry plane* by John Foster © 2000, John Foster (2000, Oxford University Press); 'Silver Aeroplane' by John Foster from *The Works* chosen by Paul Cookson © 2000, John Foster (2000, Macmillan) and 'Swaying in the breeze' from *The Poetry Quest* by John Foster © 2000, John Foster (2000, Oxford University Press). **Harper Collins Publishers** and Frank R Williamson and Christopher R Tolkien, executors of the Estate of the late J R R Tolkien for extracts from *The Hobbit* by JRR Tolkien © 1937, JRR Tolkien (1937, George Allen & Unwin Ltd). **Sheila Hoeman** for 'Doodlebugs' by Sheila Hoeman from *50 Shared Texts: Non-Fiction* by Jillian Powell © 2007, Sheila Hoeman (2007, Scholastic). **Shelagh McGee** for 'Wanted - a witch's cat' from *What do witches do and other poems* by Shelagh McGee © 1980, Shelagh McGee (1980, Prentice Hall). **David Orme** for 'An old cat is annoyed by a dove' by David Orme from *The Works* chosen by Paul Cookson © 2000, David Orme (2000, Macmillan) and 'A more detailed look at metaphor' adapted from an idea by David Orme. **Oxford University Press** for text and illustrations from *Gregory Cool* by Caroline Binch © 1994, Caroline Binch (1994, Oxford University Press). **Campbell Perry** for 'Making Mountains' and 'Spiders' Silk and Webs' by Campbell Perry from *50 Shared Text: Non-Fiction Year 4* by Jillian Powell © 2007, Campbell Perry (2007, Scholastic). **Penguin Group UK** for print use of illustrations from *Fantastic Mr Fox* by Roald Dahl, illustrated by Quentin Blake © 1996, Quentin Blake (1996, Puffin). **Saviour Pirotta** for an extract from *The Fly-by-Night* by Saviour Pirotta © 1990, Saviour Pirotta (1990, William Collins Sons & Co Ltd). **Random House Group** for the cover of *Rose Blanche* translated by Ian McEwan © 1985, Random House, and for an extract from *Beyond the Deepwoods* by Paul Stewart and Chris Riddell © 1998, Paul Stewart and Chris Riddell (1998, Doubleday). **Redwings Horse Sanctuary** for an advertisement from *Young Redwings* © 2008, Redwings Horse Sanctuary (2008, Redwings). **Rising Stars UK** for an extract from *Bunda's Dreamings* by Jay Matthews © 2007, Jay Matthews (2007, Scholastic). **Rogers, Coleridge & White** for an extract from *Rose Blanche*, text by Ian McEwan based on a story by Christopher Gallaz © 1985, Ian McEwan (1985, Editions 24 heures). **Royal Society for the Protection of Birds** for *Welcome to the RSPB Kids!* © 2008, RSPB (www.rspb.org.uk/youth). **Royal Society for the Prevention of Cruelty to Animals** for the *Trapped Terrier Rescue* photographs © 2008, Boris Lasserre (www.rspca.co.uk). **The Literacy Trustees of Walter de la Mare** and the **Society of Authors** for 'Five little eyes' by Walter de la Mare © 1969, Walter de la Mare (1969, Faber and Faber). **Angela Topping** for the 'Yo Yo!' by Angela Topping from *The Works* chosen by Paul Cookson © 2000, Angela Topping (2000, Macmillan). **A P Watt** for illustrations by Quentin Blake from *Fantastic Mr Fox* by Roald Dahl © 1961, Quentin Blake (1961, Penguin). **Chris Webster** for 'Beat the Bully' from *100 Literacy Hours: Year 3* by Chris Webster © 1993, Chris Webster (1993, Scholastic). **Bernard Young** for 'Birds of a Feather' from *Brilliant* by Bernard Young © 2000, Bernard Young (2000, Kingston Press).

Every effort has been made to trace copyright holders for the works reproduced in this book, and the publishers apologise for any inadvertent omissions.

Text © 2009, Sylvia Clements
© 2009, Scholastic Ltd

Designed using Adobe InDesign

Published by Scholastic Ltd
Villiers House
Clarendon Avenue
Leamington Spa
Warwickshire CV32 5PR

Visit our website at
www.scholastic.co.uk

Printed by Bell and Bain Ltd
123456789 9012345678

British Library Cataloguing-in-Publication Data
A catalogue record for this book is available from the British Library.
ISBN 978-1407-10186-6

Contents

100 Literacy Assessment Lessons: Year 4

'Assessment' refers to all those activities undertaken by teachers, and by their students in assessing themselves, which provide information to be used as feedback to modify the teaching and learning activities in which they are engaged.'

from Black and William *Inside the Black Box*

About the series

100 Literacy Assessment Lessons is a response to the Assessment for Learning strategy (AfL) and Assessing Pupils' Progress (APP) and contains all new, stand-alone material. The lessons mirror the guidelines and viewpoints of the revised approach to assessment. The CD-ROMs provide appropriate and exciting texts and a variety of assessment activities from photocopiable pages for individual, whole-class or group work to stimulating interactive activities. Together, the books and CD-ROMs will be an invaluable resource to help you understand and implement the revised approach to assessment.

About assessment

The key points of the revised approach to assessment are as follows:
- Assessments are accurate and linked to National Curriculum levels;
- Assessments are targeted, with assessment focuses used as the guiding criteria;
- Assessments are reliable and based on a range of evidence;
- Assessments are useful and appropriate: day to day, periodic or transitional.

Type of assessment	Purpose	Strategies
Day to day	Ongoing and formative: encourages reflection and informs the next steps in teaching and learning.	Objectives, outcomes and success criteria are made explicit and are shared with children; observations are used to gather evidence; peer assessment and self-assessment help to develop children as responsible learners.
Periodic	Provides a periodic view of children's progress and diagnostic information linked to national standards.	Progress and attainment are reviewed regularly (half-termly or termly) against APP criteria; strengths and gaps in learning are identified to inform future planning.
Transitional	Brings together evidence, including tests, at points of transition (eg level to level or year to year); provides a formal overview of children's attainment set within the framework of national standards.	Use of formal tasks and tests; external validation and reporting.

For a complete list of strategies for day-to-day assessment and further information about periodic and transitional assessment, visit the National Strategies website (**http://nationalstrategies.standards.dcsf.gov.uk**).

What are assessment focuses (AFs)?

Assessment focuses (AFs) are tools for assessment that sit between the National Curriculum programmes of study and level descriptions. The AFs provide more detailed criteria against which children's standards of attainment can be assessed and judged.

About the book

Reflecting the structure of the renewed Primary Framework for Literacy (2006), the book is divided into three Blocks: Narrative, Non-fiction and Poetry. Each Block is further divided into Units, and the Units are split into Phases. The Phases are divided into a number of day-to-day assessment activities. These assessment activities, based on learning outcomes, are designed to fit easily into your existing planning.

Units

Each Unit covers a different text-type or genre and, because of this, each Unit has its own introduction containing the following:

Literacy objectives: All objectives for the Unit are listed under their strand names.

Key aspects of learning: Aspects of learning that the Unit covers are identified from the renewed Primary National Strategy (PNS) Framework.

Assessment focuses (AFs): The main assessment focuses that are addressed during the Unit are listed from APP.

Speaking and listening: Assessment areas you should look out for are linked to the Speaking and listening strand objectives.

Resources: Lists all of the resources required for the activities in each Phase.

Planning grids: There are two grids per Unit to provide an overview of the Unit and to suggest how you can build assessment opportunities into your medium-term planning. The grids show Phases, learning outcomes, a summary of lessons, assessment opportunities and potential evidence, levelled statements of the assessment focuses (AFs), and success criteria matched to the learning outcomes in the form of 'I can...' statements.

Assessment activities

Each assessment activity follows the same format:

Learning outcomes: These are relevant to individual activities or a set of activities that share objectives.

Success criteria: These are child-friendly 'I can...' statements for children or teachers to refer to during or following the activity.

Setting the context: This section provides guidance on what the task is and details the children's expected prior learning. The context for the task may also be explained: group, paired or individual work. Where adult support is required, this is also described.

Assessment opportunity: This section highlights what to assess, how to find out what children know, and what questions to ask.

Assessment evidence: This section suggests what to look for during an activity in relation to specific assessment focuses (AFs).

Next steps: This section is divided into support and extension. It provides ideas to enable children to revisit an objective or learning outcome, and gives feedback or targets to move children forward, consolidate or extend their learning.

Key aspects of learning: Key aspects of learning are linked to specific activities.

Photocopiable pages

At the end of each Unit is a selection of photocopiable activity pages. The full range of these is provided on the CD-ROM, including levelled versions where appropriate. Photocopiable pages may include self-assessment statements for ticking as well as a 'traffic light' system for colouring (see 'Self-assessment' on page 7 for more information.) Where 'I can...' statements are not included, peer assessment may be suggested within an activity.

Transitional assessment

Also included on the CD-ROM are some SATs-style formal single-level assessments. More information about these can be found on page 7, and a grid detailing their content is provided on page 174.

How to use the materials

The activities in the book provide a balance of whole-class/group/paired/independent learning and teaching, and give the opportunity not only for day-to-day assessment but also for collection of evidence against individual assessment focuses (AFs) for periodic review. Each activity can be slotted into a lesson where appropriate and may involve discussion work, written responses, use of photocopiable pages or interactive activities.

Two periodic assessment activities are provided at the end of each Unit – one for reading and one for writing. The focus of each of these activities is usually a photocopiable page that assesses children on the learning outcomes covered during the Unit and provides further evidence against the assessment focuses. You can also use these periodic assessments to help you to make level judgements that match to the Reading and Writing Attainment Targets (ATs).

Making a level judgement

Assessment involves making a level judgement against national standards at regular intervals. The following steps will support you in adopting a strategic approach to the marking and levelling needed for assessment.

Step one: Consider evidence
● Use a range of appropriate evidence to make a level judgement, for example, written or oral;
● Remember that it is quality not quantity that matters;
● Keep examples of children's work that will provide significant evidence.

Step two: Review the evidence
● Take a broader view of a child's achievement across the whole subject and over time;
● Create a visual picture of strengths and learning gaps by highlighting criteria a child has met across a range of evidence;
● Collaborate with colleagues and agree what constitutes success for the various assessment criteria.

Step three: Make a judgement
● Consult the English Assessment Guidelines (see National Standards website: **http://nationalstrategies.standards.dcsf.gov.uk** and look at exemplar material provided in the Standards files;
● Arrive at an overall subject level judgement;
● Think about what the child demonstrates:
  – How much of the level;
  – How consistently;
  – How independently;
  – In what range of contexts.
● Finally, fine-tune your levelling to 'high', 'secure' or 'low'.

What's on the CD-ROM?

Each CD-ROM contains a wealth of resources. These include:
● **Photocopiable pages:** levelled where appropriate, including text extracts and activity sheets for day-to-day and periodic assessment.
● **Transitional assessments:** single-level tests for levels 2–5 including mark schemes and instructions.
● **Interactive activities:** for individuals or small groups, with in-built marking to assess specific learning outcomes.
● **Whiteboard tools:** a set of tools (including a pen, highlighter, eraser, notes and reward stickers) that can be used to annotate activity sheets or interactive activities. These tools will work on any interactive whiteboard or conventional screen.
● **Editable planning grids** (in Word format) are available to help teachers integrate the assessment activities into their medium-term and weekly planning.

How to use the CD-ROM

System requirements
Minimum specification:
- PC or Mac with a CD-ROM drive and 512 Mb RAM (recommended)
- Windows 98SE or above/Mac OS X.4 or above
- Recommended minimum processor speed: 1 GHz

Getting started
The *100 Literacy Assessment Lessons* CD-ROM should auto run when inserted into your CD drive. If it does not, browse to your CD drive to view the contents of the CD-ROM and click on the *100 Literacy Assessment Lessons* icon.

From the start-up screen you will find four options: select **Credits** to view a list of acknowledgements. Click on **Register** to register the product in order to receive product updates and special offers. Click on **How to use this CD-ROM** to access support notes for using the CD-ROM. Finally, if you agree to the terms and conditions, select **Start** to move to the main menu.

For all technical support queries, contact Scholastic Customer Services help desk on 0845 6039091.

Navigating the CD-ROM
The CD-ROM allows users to search for resources by Block or Unit, or by assessment focus. Users can also search by assessment type (day to day, periodic or transitional) or by resource type (for example, worksheet, interactive resource, or text extract).

Day-to-day assessments
These should be used to support learning. They can be used during a lesson, when you judge that children are ready for an assessment activity. The materials can also be used weekly or after a unit of work has been completed.

Periodic assessments
These can be used with a group of children rather than with the whole class. This could be at the end of a unit of work (for example, at the end of a half-term or term). Decide who is ready to be assessed using the outcomes of the day-to-day assessment activities and your observations of children's performance.

Self-assessment
There is a 'traffic light' system at the bottom of some photocopiable pages that children can shade to show how they feel about the activity: red for 'need help'; orange for 'having some understanding'; green for 'I found this easy!'. (Alternatively, you may wish to utilise these as a teacher marking tool for providing an at-a-glance guide to the child's progress.)

The photocopiable sheets also provide 'I can...' statements with tick boxes, to enable children to self-assess specifically in terms of the relevant learning outcomes/success criteria. A similar system is in place at the end of all the interactive activities, where the children are asked to click on a traffic light, and to type in any comments.

Transitional tests
These single-level tests provide evidence of where, in relation to national standards, children are at a given point in time. There are two Reading and Writing assessments for each level. Each reading assessment consists of a two-part reading comprehension test based on two different text types. Each writing assessment consists of two writing tasks – shorter and longer – that focus on writing for different purposes. All the tasks and tests for levels 2–5 are included on the CD-ROM together with easy-to-follow marking schemes (see pages 174–175 for more information.)

Class PET
A whole-school version of *100 Literacy Assessment Lessons* is available with an expanded range of digital assessment activities, as well as the facility to report, record and track children's work. For further information visit the Class PET website, **www.scholastic.co.uk/classpet**.

🔲 Periodic assessment

Unit	AT	Page	Assessment focuses	Learning outcomes
Narrative 1	Reading	20	AF2	Children will interrogate texts to deepen and clarify understanding and response.
	Writing	20	AF1, AF3, AF4, AF5	Children can write a complete narrative with their ideas organised into paragraphs.
Narrative 2	Reading	37	AF5	Children can express opinions about an author's intended impact on a reader.
	Writing	38	AF1, AF7	Children can write a description of a fantasy setting which will create mood and atmosphere, using elements of the real world to hook the reader. Children can describe a fantasy guide and create an image in the reader's mind.
Narrative 3	Reading	49	AF2, AF3, AF7	Children can read stories from other cultures. Children can discuss characters and predict how settings have an impact on behaviour.
	Writing	49	AF1, AF4, AF6	Children know how a story is organised through paragraphs and connectives. Children can discuss characters and predict how settings have an impact on behaviour.
Narrative 4	Reading	64	AF2, AF3, AF6	Children can identify how an opening paragraph can introduce a main character and trigger an issue.
	Writing	64	AF1	Children can write an opening to a story with an issue using a trigger point.
Narrative 5	Reading	79	AF2, AF3	Children can develop a playscript from a piece of narrative.
	Writing	79	AF2	Children can develop a playscript from a piece of narrative.
Non-fiction 1	Reading	94	AF2, AF3	Children can record evidence for a newspaper article based on a range of evidence sources.
	Writing	95	AF1–AF8	Children can plan, draft and publish a newspaper article using the appropriate language and presentational features.
Non-fiction 2	Reading	109	AF2, AF4	Children can understand the features of information books.
	Writing	109	AF2, AF3, AF4, AF7	Children can develop notes into paragraphs of written text using the features of information texts.

Unit	AT	Page	Assessment focuses	Learning outcomes
Non-fiction 3	Reading	125	AF2, AF4	Children can create a flow diagram of a written explanation.
	Writing	125	AF2, AF3	Children can write an explanation text from a diagrammatic plan using the conventions of the text type.
Non-fiction 4	Reading	140	AF4, AF6	Children can identify key language features in paper-based persuasive texts.
	Writing	140	AF2, AF7	Children can write a persuasive text using informal language and a range of devices used to persuade.
Poetry 1	Reading	153	AF4, AF5, AF6	Children will recognise and discuss how poets use language (including similes and metaphors and other simple images) to create a vivid picture in words.
	Writing	154	AF7	Children can paint a vivid word picture using similes and other simple images.
Poetry 2	Reading	170	AF1, AF4	Children look for and use some technical terms in discussion of poems. Children can explain how writers have used expressive and figurative language for impact and effect.
	Writing	170	AF1, AF3	Children can write a poem about the seasons using a form of their choice. Children can use ICT to present their poem creatively.

PERIODIC

NARRATIVE

UNIT 1 Stories with historical settings

Literacy objectives

Speak and listen for a wide range of purposes in different contexts
Strand 1 Speaking
- Tell stories effectively and convey detailed information coherently for listeners.

Strand 2 Listening and responding
- Compare the different contributions of music, words and images in short extracts from TV programmes.

Read and write for a range of purposes on paper and on screen
Strand 7 Understanding and interpreting texts
- Deduce characters' reasons for behaviour from their actions and explain how ideas are developed in non-fiction texts.

Strand 8 Engaging with and responding to texts
- Interrogate texts to deepen and clarify understanding and response.

Strand 9 Creating and shaping texts
- Develop and refine ideas in writing using planning and problem-solving strategies.
- Use settings and characterisation to engage readers' interest.

Strand 10 Text structure and organisation
- Organise text into paragraphs to distinguish between different information, events or processes.

Strand 12 Presentation
- Use word-processing packages to present written work and continue to increase speed and accuracy in typing.

Key aspects of learning

Creative thinking
- Children will be encouraged to use their historical knowledge and their imaginations to create a setting and a new story set in the past.

Empathy
- Exploring historical settings and events through narrative will help children to develop a sense of empathy with historical characters and an understanding of their way of life.

Self-awareness
- Children will discuss and reflect on their personal responses to the texts.

Communication
- Children will often work collaboratively in pairs and groups. They will communicate outcomes orally, in writing and using other modes and media where appropriate.

Assessment focuses

Reading

AF2 (*understand, describe, select or retrieve information, events or ideas from texts and use quotation and reference to text*).

AF3 (*deduce, infer or interpret information, events or ideas from texts*).

AF4 (*identify and comment on the structure and organisation of texts, including grammatical and presentational features at text level*).

AF5 (*explain and comment on writers' use of language, including grammatical and literary features at word and sentence level*).

AF7 (*relate texts to their social, cultural and historical contexts and literary traditions*).

Writing

AF1 (*write imaginative, interesting and thoughtful texts*).

AF3 (*organise and present whole texts effectively, sequencing and structuring information, ideas and events*).

AF5 (*vary sentences for clarity, purpose and effect*).

AF6 (*write with technical accuracy of syntax and punctuation in phrases, clauses and sentences*).

Speaking and listening

Speaking (speak with clarity, intonation and pace).

Listening and responding (listen to a speaker and recall relevant information).

Resources

Phase 1 activities
The War and Freddy by Dennis Hamley (ISBN 978-0590-55866-2)
Rose Blanche by Roberto Innocenti (ISBN 978-0224-02841-7)
Photocopiable pages, 'Character sketches' (versions 1 and 2)
Interactive activity, 'Character sketches'
Phase 2 activities
Photocopiable pages, 'Story map' (versions 1 and 2)
Photocopiable page, 'Powerful verbs'
Interactive activity, 'Powerful verbs'
Phase 3 activities
Photocopiable page, 'Story planning'
Periodic assessment
Interactive activity, 'Narrative 1 Reading assessment text'
Photocopiable page, 'Narrative 1 Reading assessment'

Unit 1 📖 Stories with historical settings

Learning outcomes	Assessment opportunity and evidence	Assessment focuses (AFs)		Success criteria
		Level 2	Level 3	
Phase ① activities pages 15–16				
Set in the past Children can read stories with a historical setting and find evidence about the period when the story is set.	• Shared reading and group discussion of two WWII stories. • Children's verbal responses and teacher's notes.	**Reading AF7** • General features of a few text types identified. • Some awareness that books are set in different times and places.	**Reading AF7** • Some simple connections between texts identified. • Recognition of some features of the context of texts.	• I can identify features of stories set in the past. • I can make notes to support my hypotheses.
Character sketches Children can write character sketches using evidence deduced from the text.	• Independent activity where children match Rose Blanche's actions to descriptive words and phrases. • Completed photocopiable page and written character sketches for Rose Blanche.	**Reading AF3** • Simple, plausible inference about events and information, using evidence from text. • Comments based on textual cues, sometimes misunderstood. **Writing AF6** • Clause structure mostly grammatically correct. • Sentence demarcation with capital letters and full stops usually accurate. • Some accurate use of question and exclamation marks, and commas in lists.	**Reading AF3** • Straightforward inference based on a single point of reference in the text. • Responses to text show meaning established at a literal level. **Writing AF6** • Straightforward sentences usually demarcated accurately with full stops, capital letters, question and exclamation marks. • Some, limited, use of speech punctuation. • Comma splicing evident, particular in narrative.	• I can find evidence from the text that describes a character. • I can write a character description using evidence from the text.
Phase ② activities pages 17–18				
Story map Children can recognise the stages in a story and the way that events are linked.	• Supported activity where children sequence sentences into the correct stages on a story map. • Completed story maps for Rose Blanche.	**Reading AF4** Some awareness of use of features of organisation.	**Reading AF4** A few basic features of organisation at text level identified, with little or no linked comment.	• I can identify the structure of a story (introduction, build-up, problem, climax, ending). • I can talk about how the stages of a story link together.
Powerful verbs Children can identify powerful verbs in a text and can talk about their function.	• Independent activity where children identify powerful verbs using an interactive activity. • Completed interactive activity and teacher's notes.	**Reading AF5** • Some effective language choices noted. • Some familiar patterns of language identified.	**Reading AF5** A few basic features of writer's use of language identified, but with little or no comment.	I can find powerful verbs in a story.
Phase ③ activities pages 18–19				
Story planning Children can plan a story with a clear structure including a build-up, climax or conflict, and resolution.	• Paired discussion about WWII photographs. • Independent activity where children plan a story using photocopiable page. • Completed story plans.	**Writing AF3** • Some basic sequencing of ideas or material. • Openings and/or closings sometimes signalled.	**Writing AF3** • Some attempt to organise ideas with related points placed next to each other. • Openings and closings usually signalled. • Some attempt to sequence ideas or material logically.	• I can use photographs to give me ideas for my story setting and characters. • I can use a planning board to plan a story in five stages.
The passage of time Children can use connectives to show changes in time or place and the sequence of events.	• Whole-class activity where children brainstorm a list of time connectives. • Children's oral responses and completed story plans.	**Writing AF3** • Some basic sequencing of ideas or material. • Openings and/or closings sometimes signalled.	**Writing AF3** • Some attempt to organise ideas with related points placed next to each other. • Openings and closings usually signalled. • Some attempt to sequence ideas or material logically.	I can use time connectives to show the passage of time in my story plan.

Unit 1 📖 Stories with historical settings

Learning outcomes	Assessment opportunity and evidence	Assessment focuses (AFs)		Success criteria
		Level 4	Level 5	
Phase ① activities pages 15-16				
Set in the past Children can read stories with a historical setting and find evidence about the period when the story is set.	• Shared reading and group discussion of two WWII stories. • Children's verbal responses and teacher's notes.	**Reading AF7** • Features common to different texts or versions of the same text identified, with simple comment. • Simple comment on the effect that the reader's or writer's context has on the meaning of texts.	**Reading AF7** • Comments identify similarities and differences between texts, or versions, with some explanation. • Some explanation of how the contexts in which texts are written and read contribute to meaning.	• I can identify features of stories set in the past. • I can make notes to support my hypotheses.
Character sketches Children can write character sketches using evidence deduced from the text.	• Independent activity where children refer to the evidence from the text *Rose Blanche* to help them to write a character sketch. • Written character sketches.	**Reading AF3** • Comments make inferences based on evidence from different points in the text. • Inferences often correct, but comments are not always rooted securely in the text or repeat narrative or content. **Writing AF6** • Sentences demarcated accurately throughout the text, including question marks. • Speech marks to denote speech generally accurate, with some other speech punctuation. • Commas used in lists and occasionally to mark clauses, although not always accurate.	**Reading AF3** • Comments develop explanation of inferred meanings drawing on evidence across the text. • Comments make inferences and deductions based on textual evidence. **Writing AF6** • Full range of punctuation used accurately to demarcate sentences, including speech punctuation. • Syntax and punctuation within the sentence generally accurate including commas to mark clauses, though some errors occur where ambitious structures are attempted.	• I can find evidence from the text that describes a character. • I can write a character description using evidence from the text.
Phase ② activities pages 17-18				
Story map Children can recognise the stages in a story and the way that events are linked.	• Independent activity where children organise their writing into stages on a story map. • Completed story maps for *Rose Blanche*.	**Reading AF4** Some basic features of organisation at text level identified.	**Reading AF4** Various features relating to organisation at text level, including form, are clearly identified.	• I can identify the structure of a story (introduction, build-up, problem, climax, ending). • I can talk about how the stages of a story link together.
Powerful verbs Children can identify powerful verbs in a text and can talk about their function.	• Independent activity where children identify powerful verbs in a story extract and explain why they have been used. • Highlighted story extracts and completed photocopiable pages.	**Reading AF5** • Some basic features of writer's use of language identified. • Simple comments on writer's choices.	**Reading AF5** • Various features of writer's use of language identified, with some explanation. • Comments show some awareness of the effect of writer's language choices.	I can find powerful verbs in a story.
Phase ③ activities pages 18-19				
Story planning Children can plan a story with a clear structure including a build-up, climax or conflict, and resolution.	• Paired discussion about WWII photographs. • Independent activity where children plan a story using photocopiable page. • Completed story plans.	**Writing AF3** • Ideas organised by clustering related points or by time sequence. • Ideas are organised simply with a fitting opening and closing, sometimes linked. • Ideas or material generally in logical sequence but overall direction of writing not always clearly signalled.	**Writing AF3** • Material is structured clearly, with sentences organised into appropriate paragraphs. • Development of material is effectively managed across text. • Overall direction of the text supported by clear links between paragraphs.	• I can use photographs to give me ideas for my story setting and characters. • I can use a planning board to plan a story in five stages.

📕 SCHOLASTIC   100 LITERACY ASSESSMENT LESSONS • YEAR 4   13

Unit 1 🔲 Stories with historical settings

Learning outcomes	Assessment opportunity and evidence	Assessment focuses (AFs)		Success criteria
		Level 4	Level 5	
Phase ③ activities pages 18–19				
The passage of time Children can use connectives to show changes in time or place and the sequence of events.	● Whole-class activity where children brainstorm a list of time connectives. ● Children's oral responses and completed story.	**Writing AF3** ● Ideas organised by clustering related points or by time sequence. ● Ideas are organised simply with a fitting opening and closing, sometimes linked. ● Ideas or material generally in logical sequence but overall direction of writing not always clearly signalled.	**Writing AF3** ● Material is structured clearly, with sentences organised into appropriate paragraphs. ● Development of material is effectively managed across text, eg. closings refer back to openings. ● Overall direction of the text supported by clear links between paragraphs.	I can use time connectives to show the passage of time in my story plan.

Phase ① Set in the past

Learning outcome
Children can read stories with a historical setting and find evidence about the period when the story is set.

Success criteria
● I can identify features of stories set in the past.
● I can make notes to support my hypotheses.

Setting the context
This activity takes two stories set in the Second World War as its context and so assumes that the children will have some knowledge of this period. Tell the whole class that you are going to read them two stories set in the past. Explain that as you read, they should make notes of any features that tell them the stories are set in the past: historical events, vocabulary, clothes, descriptions and so on. Remind the children that the illustrations may also provide evidence. Read the first chapter of *The War and Freddy* and then the whole of the story *Rose Blanche*.

Assessment opportunity
Allow time after reading the texts for the children to complete their notes. Share the children's findings and discuss how the stories are both set in the Second World War. Divide the children into discussion groups, split by ability. Invite them to tell you what evidence they found and to give reasons. Ask questions such as *Why do the trains tell you that the story is in the past?* Challenge the more confident group to make connections between the two stories. Record the children's verbal responses and evaluate their responses against the success criteria.

Assessment evidence
At levels 2–3, children will identify simple features such as gas masks, call-up and rations. At levels 4–5, children will use their historical knowledge to make comparisons between the stories. For example, they may comment that *The War and Freddy* is written from the point of view of an English child whereas *Rose Blanche* is written from the point of view of a German child. This activity will provide evidence towards Reading AF7.

Next steps
Support: Provide children with another appropriate text that contains historical features, and a highlighter pen. Read the text slowly while the children follow. Stop at each sentence and invite them to give examples of evidence and to go back and highlight the words.
Extension: Provide children with a more challenging book set in a similar historical period. Invite them to find evidence in the text that indicates the historical period. Encourage them to discuss how the author develops the sense of time setting.

Key aspects of learning
Empathy: Exploring historical settings and events through narrative will help children to develop a sense of empathy with historical characters and an understanding of their way of life.

NARRATIVE

Phase ① Character sketches

Learning outcome
Children can write character sketches using evidence deduced from the text.

Success criteria
- I can find evidence from the text that describes a character.
- I can write a character description using evidence from the text.

Setting the context
The children should have had previous experience of character analysis: through discussion, drama or writing activities. They should know that character traits are presented through examples of behaviour and dialogue. Re-read *Rose Blanche* and invite the children to identify evidence that tells them about Rose, the main character. Brainstorm a list of adjectives or descriptive phrases that describe Rose, ensuring coverage of those on the photocopiable pages 'Character sketches' (versions 1 and 2).

Assessment opportunity
Children working at levels 2–3 can work independently, using version 1 of the photocopiable page 'Character sketches' or the interactive activity 'Character sketches' to match adjectives and descriptive phrases to Rose's actions. They should then use this learning to write their own character sketch of Rose on a separate sheet. Children working at levels 4–5 can use version 2 of the photocopiable page to write a character sketch. Encourage them to refer to the text to back up their choice of adjectives and descriptive phrases. Ask them to explain their choices and assess their responses. While the children are writing, observe their ability to punctuate sentences accurately.

Assessment evidence
At levels 2–3, children who can match adjectives and descriptive phrases to evidence from the text will demonstrate an ability to carry out simple inference. In their writing they may punctuate simple sentences accurately with full stops and capital letters. At levels 4–5, children will infer meaning and make deductions that draw on evidence from different parts of the story. They will also use a wider range of punctuation in their writing including commas and speech marks. This activity will provide evidence towards Reading AF3 and Writing AF6.

Next steps
Support: Work in a guided reading group with a number of prepared labels detailing character traits. Discuss what each means, for example: *What sort of things might someone do if they were brave?* As you read your chosen text together invite the children to pick up labels if they hear something that tells them that the character has done something to match that trait.
Extension: Develop children's ability to infer by asking them to discuss and predict Rose's actions in different situations. For example: *What do you think Rose would have done if she had managed to hide an escaped prisoner? How would she have reacted if she had been caught and questioned?*

Key aspects of learning
Empathy: Exploring historical settings and events through narrative will help children to develop a sense of empathy with historical characters and an understanding of their way of life.
Self-awareness: Children will discuss and reflect on their personal responses to the texts.
Communication: Children will often work collaboratively in pairs and groups. They will communicate outcomes orally, in writing and using other modes and media where appropriate.

Phase ② Story map

Learning outcome
Children can recognise the stages in a story and the way that events are linked.

Success criteria
● I can identify the structure of a story (introduction, build-up, problem, climax, ending).
● I can talk about how the stages of a story link together.

Setting the context
Ensure the children are aware of the main stages of a story – the introduction (characters and setting are introduced), the build-up (events occur which will lead to the main problem), the problem (a dilemma occurs which causes the main character to carry out actions and these actions lead to the climax), the climax (an exciting and significant event occurs before the ending), the resolution/ending (the story draws to a close as a result of the climax, and the ending is tied back to the beginning of the story and is neatly finished). Explain that they are going to break down the story of *Rose Blanche* into the different stages and write a story plan.

Assessment opportunity
Give the children working at levels 2–3 version 1 of the photocopiable page 'Story map'. Ask them to organise the sentences into a sequence and then to decide which stage of the story each sentence represents. They could then write some of the statements into the boxes on version 2 of the photocopiable page. Give the children working at levels 4–5 version 2 of the photocopiable page to record their own ideas about how the story of *Rose Blanche* breaks down into stages. Encourage them to explain how the stages are linked, for example: 'In the introduction we learn about Rose's daily routines, and in the build-up she is carrying out these routines when she witnesses the boy attempting an escape.'

Assessment evidence
At levels 2–3, children will demonstrate that they can organise part of the story into stages and in particular will recognise the beginning and ending. At levels 4–5, children will outline the events at each stage of the story and comment on how they are linked. The completed story plans will provide evidence towards Reading AF4.

Next steps
Support: If children struggle with identifying the stages, simplify the story plan into beginning, middle and end. Sort the sentences into these three stages before breaking the story down further to demonstrate how to identify the build-up, problem and climax.
Extension: Have children work in a discussion group to produce a generic Story Plan Help Sheet explaining what they would include in each stage of a story. Prompt children to explain how they could ensure that they create vivid setting descriptions. How would they ensure the story has a neat ending?

Key aspects of learning
Self-awareness: Children will discuss and reflect on their personal responses to the texts.

NARRATIVE

Phase ② Powerful verbs

Learning outcome
Children can identify powerful verbs in a text and can talk about their function.

Success criteria
I can find powerful verbs in a story.

Setting the context
The children will have carried out sentence-level work on verbs and verb tenses. They will know how to recognise a verb or verb phrase in a sentence and will understand its function. They will also know what is meant by a 'powerful verb' and why it would be used. Re-read the last two pages of *Rose Blanche* to the class. Explain to them that they will need to work independently to identify the verbs in the passage from *Rose Blanche*.

Assessment opportunity
Ask children working at levels 2–3 to identify all the verbs in the text extract using the first screen of the interactive activity 'Powerful verbs'. They should then re-read the passage from the second screen but this time only highlight the verbs that are powerful. Ask children working at levels 4–5 to read the text extract from the photocopiable page 'Powerful verbs' and to underline all the verbs. They can then highlight the powerful verbs, back up their choice of verbs with definitions and say why they think the author chose the verbs. Observe whether all the children can identify the phrasal verbs: 'went by', 'put on', 'took up' and 'had triumphed'.

Assessment evidence
At levels 2–3, children will highlight some powerful verbs in the sentences. At levels 4–5, children will identify the powerful verbs, give meanings and provide reasons for their choices. The completed activity will provide evidence towards Reading AF5.

Next steps
Support: Provide children with simple sentences, for example, 'The boy went across the road.' Invite them to highlight the verb and then discuss alternative choices using more powerful verbs, for example, 'The boy *dashed* across the road.'
Extension: Provide children with a list of simple verbs. Children can use a thesaurus to build a bank of alternative powerful verbs to draw on when writing their Evacuee Story (see Periodic Writing assessment on page 20).

Key aspects of learning
Communication: Children will communicate outcomes orally, in writing and using other modes and media where appropriate.

Phase ③ Story planning

Learning outcome
Children can plan a story with a clear structure including a build-up, climax or conflict, and resolution.

Success criteria
● I can use photographs to give me ideas for my story setting and characters.
● I can use a planning board to plan a story in five stages.

Setting the context
This activity assumes that children can identify and map the main stages of a story. Children will also need to know facts about evacuation during the Second World War. If not already taught as part of a history scheme, use online resources or TV programmes to provide information. Hand out the photocopiable page, 'Story planning', which is a blank story plan with each stage supported by a photograph (a poster informing parents to evacuate their children from London, children waiting at a train station, children on the train leaving the city, children waiting to be picked by host families, children settling into their new homes in the countryside).

📕SCHOLASTIC

Assessment opportunity

Arrange the children into 'talk partners'. Ask them to discuss each photograph in the context of the stages of a narrative about evacuation. Come together as a class to agree a skeleton story plan. Prompt children to consider who the story is about, why children are being evacuated, who they are leaving behind, how they feel and what they do to show their feelings ('She clutched her teddy tightly.'). Ask the children to plan their narrative, individually, using the photocopiable page, 'Story planning'.

Assessment evidence

At levels 2-3, children will organise some ideas for their story into a basic sequence and will attempt to place related points next to each other. At levels 4-5, children will organise their ideas by clustering related points and their plans will generally have a logical sequence. This activity will provide evidence for Writing AF3.

Next steps

Support: For children who struggle to plan each stage of their story, ask them to first retell the story orally and then work with them to develop their story plan and add to it through the use of prompt questions.
Extension: Ask children to add to their plans powerful verbs, actions to show character traits and possible dialogue for their final written piece.

Key aspects of learning

Creative thinking: Children will be encouraged to use their historical knowledge and their imaginations to create a setting and a new story set in the past.

Phase ③ The passage of time

Learning outcome
Children can use connectives to show changes in time or place and the sequence of events.

Success criteria

I can use time connectives to show the passage of time in my story plan.

Setting the context

The children will need to have completed the story plans from the previous activity above. They will understand the term 'connective' and know that time connectives help the reader to understand how much time has passed between events.

Assessment opportunity

Brainstorm time connectives with the whole class - individual words and phrases which show the passage of time: 'finally', 'early one morning', 'as soon as', 'later that day', 'some months later' and so on. From the list of connectives, ask the children to select the ones they will use in each stage of their story and to write these on to their story plans at the relevant stages. Record the children's oral responses.

Assessment evidence

At levels 2-3, children may note some connective words in sections of their story plans but they are more likely to link these sections by use of pronouns. At levels 4-5, they will note down connective words and phrases on their plans in a clear and logical sequence. The completed activity will provide evidence towards Writing AF3.

Next steps

Support: If children do not make appropriate suggestions ask questions to help them to consider which connectives to use: *How could we describe how long the train journey took? How long did it seem that they had been away from home?*
Extension: Encourage children to develop creative connective phrases, for example, 'as Winter blossomed into Spring...'.

Key aspects of learning

Creative thinking: Children will be encouraged to use their historical knowledge and their imaginations to create a setting and a new story set in the past.

NARRATIVE

Periodic assessment

Reading

Learning outcome Children will interrogate texts to deepen and clarify understanding and response.	**Success criteria** I can read a text to find evidence about the period when the story is set.

Setting the context
Explain to the children that, before writing their extended narrative, they are going to find out extra historical information about evacuation during the Second World War.

Assessment opportunity
Ask the children to independently explore five hot spots in the photograph from the interactive activity 'Narrative 1 Reading assessment text', in order to answer the questions on the photocopiable page 'Narrative 1 Reading assessment'. Observe how the children navigate the text and their ability to extract relevant information. Use the interactive notes to add comments to children's work.

Assessment evidence
At levels 2–3, children will retrieve some basic information from the text. At levels 4–5, children's responses will be backed up by appropriate references to the text. The children's answers and your comments will provide evidence against Reading AF2. Use this activity and evidence gathered throughout this unit to help you judge the children's overall level in Reading.

Writing

Learning outcome
Children can write a complete narrative with their ideas organised into paragraphs.

Success criteria
● I can write a historical story using my story plan.
● I can use connectives to show changes in time or place.
● I can use paragraphs to organise my ideas.
● I can use powerful verbs to create interest.

Setting the context
Explain to the children that they will use their story plans, from the Phase 3 activity, to write a complete narrative. Ensure the success criteria are clearly outlined before they start. Tell the children you are looking for a story with clear stages, presented in paragraphs, which relate to different events in the story. Some children can type their stories using a word-processing program.

Assessment opportunity
When children have completed their stories, let them self-assess, or peer-assess against the success criteria. Children can use the traffic lights to judge how well they have performed or they can highlight powerful verbs, time connectives and paragraph beginnings in their peers' work. Allow children time to edit their stories and invite them to set personal targets.

Assessment evidence
Use the completed stories to collate evidence against Writing AF1, AF3, AF4 and AF5. Look for appropriate ideas, logical organisation, use of paragraphs and sentence variation in the children's writing. Use this activity and evidence gathered throughout this unit to make level judgements for Writing.

Name	Date

Character sketches (1)

- Read the sentences below that describe Rose's actions in the story.
- Choose a word or phrase to match each sentence and to describe Rose's character.
- Now write your own character sketch on a separate sheet.

German
ordinary little girl
blonde hair
young
helpful
instinctive
caring
inquisitive
fast runner

determined
secretive
careful
unselfish
heroine
observant
brave
friendly
righteous

Rose went shopping for her mum quite a lot. _____

She played with her friends and went to school. _____

While the boy tried to escape from the lorry, Rose quietly watched from a distance. _____

Angry at how the boy was treated, Rose followed the lorry to see where it was taking the children. _____

Even though it was muddy and the branches scratched her face, she kept on going. _____

Despite the danger and the bitter cold of winter, Rose returned day after day to feed the ghost-like children. _____

She told no one of her actions. _____

Even though she was hungry herself, and getting thinner by the day, Rose gave her food to the starving prisoners. _____

Cover © 1985, Random House Group Ltd.

Red ◉
Amber ◉
Green ◉

I can find evidence from the text that describes a character. ☐

I can write a character description using evidence from the text. ☐

Name   Date

Story map (1)

- Cut out the sentences below, summarising the story of *Rose Blanche*.
- Decide which stage of the story each sentence fits into.
- Write some of the sentences into your Story map.

There was a shot.	The war was nearly over.
The German soldiers went off to war, cheering and waving.	
The camp had gone.	Spring triumphed.
Rose was never found.	Rose disappeared.
Rose saw lots of other sad faces in the lorry.	
Rose found the prison camp and saw the starving children.	
Lorries and tanks ground through the streets day and night.	
He was caught and thrown back in the lorry.	
Frightened, the people decided to leave the town.	
Frightened soldiers were everywhere in the thick fog.	
Foreign soldiers took over the town.	Flowers and grasses grew.
Food was short, but most things carried on as normal.	
Angry, she followed the lorry to see where it was taking the children.	
Rose took food to the children in secret.	
A lorry broke down and a boy tried to escape.	

Red
Amber
Green

I can identify the structure of a story
(introduction, build-up, problem, climax, ending).

Name	Date

Powerful verbs

- Read the ending of the story of *Rose Blanche.*
- Underline ALL the verbs. Now highlight the powerful verbs.
- Complete the tab~~le~~ (asking to assistant if you need to).

Rose Blanc~~he~~

As the v~~illage~~ began.

The cold re~~mained~~ ~~the~~ land.

There were ~~soldiers~~ bright new

uniforms a~~nd~~ ~~their~~ positions

and sang th~~e~~

Spring ~~had~~ ~~come~~

[handwritten note:] 26 blew up ✓

Powerful verb	Meaning	Author's reason for choosing

Translated text © 1985, Ian McEwan.

Red
Amber
Green

I can find powerful verbs in a story. ☐

NARRATIVE

UNIT 2 Stories set in imaginary worlds

Literacy objectives

Speak and listen for a wide range of purposes in different contexts
Strand 1 Speaking
● Tell stories effectively and convey detailed information coherently for listeners.
Strand 4 Drama
● Develop scripts based on improvisation.

Read and write for a range of purposes on paper and on screen
Strand 7 Understanding and interpreting texts
● Explain how writers use figurative and expressive language to create images and atmosphere.
Strand 8 Engaging with and responding to texts
● Read extensively favourite authors or genres and experiment with other types of text.
Strand 9 Creating and shaping texts
● Develop and refine ideas in writing using planning and problem-solving strategies.
● Use settings and characterisation to engage readers' interest.
● Show imagination through language used to create emphasis, humour, atmosphere or suspense.
Strand 10 Text structure and organisation
● Organise text into paragraphs to distinguish between different information, events or processes.
● Use adverbs and conjunctions to establish cohesion within paragraphs.
Strand 11 Sentence structure and punctuation
● Clarify meaning and point of view by using varied sentence structure (phrases, clauses and adverbials).
Strand 12 Presentation
● Use word-processing packages to present written work and continue to increase speed and accuracy in typing.

Key aspects of learning

Reasoning
● Children will discuss the influence of settings on characters, using evidence from the text to justify their opinions and referring to wider evidence from their own knowledge and experience.
Evaluation
● Children will discuss the success criteria they have devised to evaluate their own written work and give feedback to others.
Self-awareness
● Children will discuss and reflect on their personal responses to the texts.
Communication
● Children will often work collaboratively in pairs and groups. They will communicate outcomes orally, in writing and using other modes and media where appropriate.

Assessment focuses

Reading
AF5 (*explain and comment on writers' use of language, including grammatical and literary features at word and sentence level*).
AF7 (*relate texts to their social, cultural and historical contexts and literary traditions*).

Writing
AF1 (*write imaginative, interesting and thoughtful texts*).
AF4 (*construct paragraphs and use cohesion within and between paragraphs*).
AF7 (*select appropriate and effective vocabulary*).

Speaking and listening
Speaking (speak with clarity, intonation and pace).
Drama (improvise and sustain roles).

Resources

Phase 1 activities
Photocopiable page, 'Features of a fantasy story'
Photocopiable pages, 'Fantasy stories' (versions 1 and 2)
Beyond The Deepwoods (*The Edge Chronicles*) by Paul Stewart and Chris Riddell (ISBN 978-0552-55422-0)
Photocopiable page, 'Creating atmosphere'
Interactive activity, 'Creating atmosphere'
Photocopiable page, 'Beyond the Deepwoods'
Photocopiable pages, 'Character reactions' (versions 1 and 2)
Phase 2 activities
Photocopiable page, 'My fantasy characters'
Interactive activity, 'Fantasy characters'
Photocopiable page, 'Fantasy story plan'
Beyond The Deepwoods (*The Edge Chronicles*) by Paul Stewart and Chris Riddell (ISBN 978-0552-55422-0)
Photocopiable page, 'Building tension'
Phase 3 activities
Photocopiable page, 'Fantasy review'
Periodic assessment
Photocopiable page, 'Narrative 2 Reading assessment text'
Photocopiable page, 'Narrative 2 Reading assessment'
Photocopiable page, 'Narrative 2 Writing assessment'

Unit 2 📖 Stories set in imaginary worlds

Learning outcomes	Assessment opportunity and evidence	Assessment focuses (AFs)		Success criteria
		Level 2	Level 3	
Phase ① activities pages 29–31				
Fantasy features Children can express opinions about an author's intended impact on a reader.	• Paired activity where children identify character roles in fantasy stories. • Children's discussions; completed photocopiable pages.	**Reading AF7** • General features of a few text types identified. • Some awareness that books are set in different times and places.	**Reading AF7** • Some simple connections between texts identified. • Recognition of some features of the context of texts.	• I can identify features of a fantasy story. • I can name and talk about stories that have fantasy settings.
Creating atmosphere Children can express opinions about an author's intended impact on a reader.	• Paired activity where children highlight words and phrases that describe a setting. • Completed interactive activity; photocopiable pages; teacher's notes.	**Reading AF5** • Some effective language choices noted. • Some familiar patterns of language identified.	**Reading AF5** A few basic features of writer's use of language identified, but with little or no comment.	• I can highlight words in a story that describe the setting. • I can explain how the author sets the mood and atmosphere.
Character reactions Children can express opinions about an author's intended impact on a reader.	• Supported group activity where children locate specific information about a character in sentences from *Beyond the Deepwoods*. • Completed photocopiable pages; children's oral responses.	**Reading AF5** • Some effective language choices noted. • Some familiar patterns of language identified.	**Reading AF5** A few basic features of writer's use of language identified, but with little or no comment.	I can give examples of how an author shows how a character feels through what they say and do.
Phase ② activities pages 32–35				
Fantasy settings Children can plan a story using the organisational features of the text type.	• Paired work where children manipulate and annotate photographs to create three atmospheric story settings. • Children's annotated photographs.	**Writing AF7** • Simple, often speech-like vocabulary conveys relevant meanings. • Some adventurous word choices.	**Writing AF7** • Simple, generally appropriate vocabulary used, limited in range. • Some words selected for effect or occasion.	• I can create my own fantasy settings using a photo-editing program. • I can describe how my edited photographs create different atmospheres. • I can describe how characters will behave in different fantasy settings.
My fantasy characters Children can plan a story using the organisational features of the text type.	• Whole-class plenary where children share and review ideas for their own fantasy characters. • Completed interactive activity; children's oral responses; completed character sketches.	**Writing AF7** • Simple, often speech-like vocabulary conveys relevant meanings. • Some adventurous word choices.	**Writing AF7** • Simple, generally appropriate vocabulary used, limited in range. • Some words selected for effect or occasion.	• I can design the characters for my own fantasy story. • I can identify the characteristics of different fantasy characters.
Planning a fantasy story Children can plan a story using the organisational features of the text type.	• Paired or small group activity where children make notes for each paragraph of their stories on a story skeleton. • Completed story skeletons; children's oral responses.	**Writing AF1** • Mostly relevant ideas and content, sometimes repetitive or sparse. • Some apt word choices create interest. • Brief comments, questions about events or actions suggest viewpoint.	**Writing AF1** • Some appropriate ideas and content included. • Some attempt to elaborate on basic information or events. • Attempt to adopt viewpoint, though often not maintained or inconsistent.	• I can use a story skeleton to plan my own fantasy story. • I can decide what will be included in each paragraph to represent different events.

Unit 2 📖 Stories set in imaginary worlds

Learning outcomes	Assessment opportunity and evidence	Assessment focuses (AFs)		Success criteria
		Level 2	**Level 3**	
Building tension Children can plan a fantasy story using the organisational features of the text type.	• Independent activity where children complete a photocopiable page on building tension in a fantasy story. • Completed photocopiable pages.	**Writing AF7** • Simple, often speech-like vocabulary conveys relevant meanings. • Some adventurous word choices.	**Writing AF7** • Simple, generally appropriate vocabulary used, limited in range. • Some words selected for effect or occasion.	I can plan how to build up tension in my fantasy story.

Phase ③ activities page 36

Learning outcomes	Assessment opportunity and evidence	Level 2	Level 3	Success criteria
Writing a fantasy story Children can write a narrative using paragraphs to organise ideas maintaining cohesion within and between paragraphs.	• Paired activity where children orally retell their planned fantasy stories. • Independent activity where children write fantasy stories in five paragraphs. • Self-evaluation of writing. • Completed stories.	**Writing AF4** Ideas in sections grouped by content, some linking by simple pronouns.	**Writing AF4** • Some internal structure within sections of text. • Within paragraphs/sections, some links between sentences • Movement between paragraphs/sections sometimes disjointed	• I can write a fantasy story using separate paragraphs for each stage of my story. • I can use cohesive devices to link my paragraphs. • I can use a review chart to make sure I have included all the features of a fantasy story.

Learning outcomes	Assessment opportunity and evidence	Assessment focuses (AFs)		Success criteria
		Level 4	**Level 5**	

Phase ① activities pages 29-31

Learning outcomes	Assessment opportunity and evidence	Level 4	Level 5	Success criteria
Fantasy features Children can express opinions about an author's intended impact on a reader.	• Supported activity where children identify character roles in fantasy stories. • Children's discussions; completed photocopiable pages.	**Reading AF7** • Features common to different texts or versions of the same text identified, with simple comment. • Simple comment on the effect that the reader's or writer's context has on the meaning of texts.	**Reading AF7** • Comments identify similarities and differences between texts, or versions, with some explanation. • Some explanation of how the contexts in which texts are written and read contribute to meaning.	• I can identify features of a fantasy story. • I can name and talk about stories that have fantasy settings.
Creating atmosphere Children can express opinions about an author's intended impact on a reader.	• Paired activity where children highlight descriptive words and phrases that describe the setting from a text extract. • Highlighted text extracts; completed photocopiable pages; teacher's notes.	**Reading AF5** • Some basic features of writer's use of language identified. • Simple comments on writer's choices.	**Reading AF5** • Various features of writer's use of language identified, with some explanation. • Comments show some awareness of the effect of writer's language choices.	• I can highlight words in a story that describe the setting. • I can explain how the author sets the mood and atmosphere.
Character reactions Children can express opinions about an author's intended impact on a reader.	• Supported group activity where children locate specific information about a character in an extract from *Beyond the Deepwoods*. • Highlighted text extracts; completed photocopiable pages; teacher's notes.	**Reading AF5** • Some basic features of writer's use of language identified. • Simple comments on writer's choices.	**Reading AF5** • Various features of writer's use of language identified, with some explanation. • Comments show some awareness of the effect of writer's language choices.	I can give examples of how an author shows how a character feels through what they say and do.

Unit 2 📖 Stories set in imaginary worlds

Learning outcomes	Assessment opportunity and evidence	Assessment focuses (AFs)		Success criteria
		Level 4	Level 5	
Phase ② activities pages 32–35				
Fantasy settings Children can plan a fantasy story using the organisational features of the text type.	• Paired work where children manipulate and annotate photographs to create three atmospheric story settings. • Children's annotated photographs.	**Writing AF7** • Some evidence of deliberate vocabulary choices. • Some expansion of general vocabulary to match topic.	**Writing AF7** • Vocabulary chosen for effect. • Reasonably wide vocabulary used, though not always appropriately.	• I can create my own fantasy settings using a photo-editing program. • I can describe how my edited photographs create different atmospheres. • I can describe how characters will behave in different fantasy settings.
My fantasy characters Children can plan a story using the organisational features of the text type.	• Whole-class plenary activity where children review the characteristics of fantasy characters and share ideas for their own fantasy characters. • Completed interactive activity, children's oral responses and the completed character sketches.	**Writing AF7** • Some evidence of deliberate vocabulary choices. • Some expansion of general vocabulary to match topic.	**Writing AF7** • Vocabulary chosen for effect. • Reasonably wide vocabulary used, though not always appropriately.	• I can design the characters for my own fantasy story. • I can identify the characteristics of different fantasy characters.
Planning a fantasy story Children can plan a story using the organisational features of the text type.	• Paired or small group activity where children make notes for each paragraph of their stories on a story skeleton. • Completed story skeletons; children's oral responses.	**Writing AF1** • Relevant ideas and content chosen. • Some ideas and material developed in detail. • Straightforward viewpoint generally established and maintained.	**Writing AF1** • Relevant ideas and material developed with some imaginative detail. • Development of ideas and material appropriately shaped for selected form. • Clear viewpoint established, generally consistent, with some elaboration.	• I can use a story skeleton to plan my own fantasy story. • I can decide what will be included in each paragraph to represent different events.
Building tension Children can plan a story using the organisational features of the text type.	• Independent activity where children complete a photocopiable page about building tension in a fantasy story. • Completed photocopiable pages.	**Writing AF7** • Some evidence of deliberate vocabulary choices. • Some expansion of general vocabulary to match topic.	**Writing AF7** • Vocabulary chosen for effect. • Reasonably wide vocabulary used, though not always appropriately.	I can plan how to build up tension in my fantasy story.
Phase ③ activities page 36				
Writing a fantasy story Children can write a narrative using paragraphs to organise ideas maintaining cohesion within and between paragraphs.	• Paired activity where children orally retell their planned fantasy stories. • Independent activity where children write fantasy stories in five paragraphs. • Self-evaluation of writing. • Completed stories.	**Writing AF4** • Paragraphs/sections help to organise content. • Within paragraphs/sections, limited range of connections between sentences. • Some attempts to establish simple links between paragraphs/sections not always maintained.	**Writing AF4** • Paragraphs clearly structure main ideas across text to support purpose. • Within paragraphs/sections, a range of devices support cohesion. • Links between paragraphs/sections generally maintained across whole text.	• I can write a fantasy story using separate paragraphs for each stage of my story. • I can use cohesive devices to link my paragraphs. • I can use a review chart to make sure I have included all the features of a fantasy story.

Phase ① Fantasy features

Learning outcome
Children can express opinions about an author's intended impact on a reader.

Success criteria
- I can identify features of a fantasy story.
- I can name and talk about stories that have fantasy settings.

Setting the context
Discuss books and films that the children know which are based in fantasy worlds, for example, *The Lord of the Rings; The Lion, The Witch and the Wardrobe* and *The Edge Chronicles*. Use the photocopiable page 'Features of a fantasy story' and information from *Grammar for Writing* Part 3 Section 1 (DfEE, 2000) to review the features of fantasy stories including typical characters. Display the photocopiable page above for children to refer to during the activity.

Assessment opportunity
Children working at levels 2-3 can work in pairs to complete version 1 of the photocopiable page 'Fantasy stories'. Observe their ability to identify the roles of characters, for example, Lucy as the guide and the White Witch as the villain. Children working at levels 4-5 can complete version 2 of the photocopiable page with adult support. Encourage them to identify shared features between the fantasy stories. Ask the children: *How are these books/films that you have listed similar? How are they different?* Invite them to recall the characters from stories that they have read and to identify the roles that each character played. They should identify the journey or quest facing each main character. For stories that are set in 'two worlds', ask children to identify the trigger mechanism that allows characters to move between the two worlds. Observe and record children's verbal contributions during their discussions.

Assessment evidence
At levels 2-3, children will correctly identify books and films that are set in fantasy contexts and will be able to give some examples of characters that fulfil different roles. At levels 4-5, children will compare and contrast films and books of the same genre in terms of the features that they share. The completed activity and your observational notes will provide evidence towards Reading AF7.

Next steps
Support: Provide children with the opportunity to watch a suitable children's adventure film. Pause the film at appropriate times to point out features that are typical of the genre.
Extension: Provide children with reading suggestions for this genre that they may not have tackled yet.

Key aspects of learning
Reasoning: Children will discuss the influence of settings on characters, using evidence from the text to justify their opinions and referring to wider evidence from their own knowledge and experience.
Self-awareness: Children will discuss and reflect on their personal responses to the texts.

NARRATIVE

Phase ① Creating atmosphere

Learning outcome
Children can express opinions about an author's intended impact on a reader.

Success criteria
- I can highlight words in a story that describe the setting.
- I can explain how the author sets the mood and atmosphere.

Setting the context
Introduce the story, *Beyond the Deepwoods*, to the whole class. Explain that this is a fantasy-world story about a boy called Twig who is brought up by wood trolls, having been abandoned at birth. Finding out the truth, Twig embarks on a nightmare journey through flesh-eating trees, and meets ferocious beasts, goblins, spindlebugs and milchgrubs on his mission to discover his true identity and his destiny. Read the introduction, which describes the entire fantasy world and, if possible, show the children the picture of the Edge.

Assessment opportunity
Arrange all of the children into 'talk partners'. Children working at levels 2–3 can use the photocopiable page 'Creating atmosphere' or the interactive activity 'Creating atmosphere' to read five sentences from *Beyond the Deepwoods*. Encourage them to highlight specific words and phrases that describe the setting and to talk about the atmosphere that the words create. At levels 4-5, children can read and highlight words from the text extract from the photocopiable page 'Beyond the Deepwoods'. Prompt them with questions: *What sort of atmosphere is created? How does the author change the mood? How does the setting change half way through the excerpt?* Encourage them to discuss the effects of words the author has used and to annotate their text extract with comments. *Can you identify adjectives that create an impact? How do the words make you feel? Which of the senses does the author draw on to create an impact?* Listen to children's discussions and take notes.

Assessment evidence
At levels 2–3, children will highlight descriptive words and phrases. At levels 4-5, children will annotate their text excerpt with words to describe the impact of the descriptions on the reader, for example, 'scary' 'mysterious' or 'magical'. The completed activity and your observational notes will provide evidence towards Reading AF5.

Next steps
Support: Select excerpts from a variety of fantasy stories and read them with the children. Encourage the children to identify sentences that create atmospheric settings. Have them type up their example sentences using an ICT word-processing program and then prompt them to use on-screen tools to highlight powerful verbs, adjectives and adverbs. Printed work can be displayed around the classroom to reinforce learning.
Extension: Encourage children to read fantasy stories from their reading books and to find their own examples of setting descriptions that create atmosphere. Children can word-process their examples and display these around the classroom.

Key aspects of learning
Self-awareness: Children will discuss and reflect on their personal responses to the texts.
Communication: Children will often work collaboratively in pairs and groups. They will communicate outcomes orally, in writing and using other modes and media where appropriate.

Phase ① Character reactions

Learning outcome
Children can express opinions about an author's intended impact on a reader.

Success criteria
I can give examples of how an author shows how a character feels through what they say and do.

Setting the context
Explain that, to be effective, an author does not tell the reader what a character is feeling but shows how they are feeling through what they say and do. Children will have previously carried out the activity on creating atmospheres.

Assessment opportunity
All children will work in supported groups. Children working at levels 2–3 can use version 1 of the photocopiable page 'Character reactions' to highlight the words and phrases that show how Twig is feeling as he embarks on his journey into the Deepwoods. Can they identify the word class used? Ask the group which verbs the author uses to show the character's actions. The children should also discuss what feelings are being portrayed: scared, surprised or annoyed. Children working at levels 4–5 can re-read their previously annotated text extract from *Beyond the Deepwoods* (see activity on page 30). Ask them to highlight, in a different colour, words that indicate the character's feelings. Assess the children's ability to identify the language choices made by the author. Can they say why one verb is a better choice than another? *What does the dialogue tell you about how the character is feeling? How does the character speak the words? What impact does this have?* The children can then use version 2 of the photocopiable page 'Character reactions' to identify the feelings the language is portraying. Extend the group by asking them to identify changes in Twig's feelings and behaviour in response to the changes in the setting. They should refer back to highlighted words from the previous activity on creating atmospheres. Take notes to capture the children's verbal responses.

Assessment evidence
At levels 2–3, children will identify individual words, and phrases. At levels 4–5, children will be able to comment on the effect of the author's language choices, for example: 'the author uses the word 'shivered' to show that Twig is really cold and scared'. They may also comment on changes in the character's behaviour linked to setting. This activity and your notes will provide evidence towards Reading AF5.

Next steps
Support: Help children to develop empathy by setting up a drama group with an adult acting as scribe. Present different situations, such as a scary roller-coaster ride or standing on the edge of a cliff. Ask children to role play the scenarios, and use freeze-frame to capture their reactions, feelings and body posture. Invite them to describe how they would feel and what they would do or say in that situation. Record verbs and adverbs: '**grip** the rail **tightly**', '**peer nervously** over the edge'.
Extension: Show children short clips from films such as *Harry Potter*, which show the character reacting to a situation in a specific way. Locate the same part in the text of the novel. Challenge children to write descriptions of how the character behaves to demonstrate his or her feelings; these may include dialogue. As a follow up they can read the excerpt from the novel and compare how the author tackled the narrative compared with their own narrative.

Key aspects of learning
Reasoning: Children will discuss the influence of settings on characters, using evidence from the text to justify their opinions and referring to wider evidence from their own knowledge and experience.
Self-awareness: Children will discuss and reflect on their personal responses to the texts.
Communication: Children will often work collaboratively in pairs and groups. They will communicate outcomes orally, in writing and using other modes and media where appropriate.

NARRATIVE

Phase ② Fantasy settings

Learning outcome
Children can plan a story using the organisational features of the text type.

Success criteria
- I can create my own fantasy settings using a photo-editing program.
- I can describe how my edited photographs create different atmospheres.
- I can describe how characters will behave in different fantasy settings.

Setting the context
Children will need to have prior knowledge about fantasy story settings. They will also need to be able to use ICT photo-editing software with confidence. Remind the children how to use PhotoPlus 6 (free to download) or alternative photo-editing software. Ask them to decide on three different settings for their fantasy stories (mountains, woods or behind a waterfall, for example) and to use an image search engine to select three photographs (copyright permitting) that reflect their choices.

Assessment opportunity
All children can work in pairs to manipulate their photographs to create their desired atmospheres (red for dangerous, threatening locations; purple for calm and mystical settings, and so on). Once they have created their images, ask the children to type a selection of captions to describe the atmosphere. Extend children by asking them to add words and phrases that describe how their character will behave in response to being in the different settings. Children working at levels 4–5 can add dialogue to each of their edited photographs. Observe the children's ability to combine words and images and to select vocabulary that will engage their reader's interest. Assess the appropriateness and effectiveness of the children's vocabulary choices.

Assessment evidence
At levels 2–3, children will annotate their photographs with simple but mostly appropriate vocabulary and they will sometimes include words and phrases for effect. At levels 4–5, children will annotate photographs with a wider range of vocabulary. This activity will provide evidence towards Writing AF7.

Next steps
Support: Assist children with descriptions of their fantasy settings and how characters would feel when exploring them.
Extension: Encourage these children to create a map of their fantasy world in which to locate their photographs. They can then write a more extensive description of their fantasy world and ideas for actions within each setting.

Key aspects of learning
Communication: Children will often work collaboratively in pairs and groups. They will communicate outcomes orally, in writing and using other modes and media where appropriate.

■ SCHOLASTIC

Phase ② My fantasy characters

Learning outcome
Children can plan a story using the organisational features of the text type.

Success criteria
- I can design the characters for my own fantasy story.
- I can identify the characteristics of different fantasy characters.

Setting the context
Recap on the different characters in well-known fantasy stories and the roles they play (refer back to the Phase 1 activity on page 29 in which fantasy features were described). Ask the children to work independently to create and describe their own fantasy characters using the photocopiable page 'My fantasy characters' to help them. They will then present their characters during the whole-class plenary.

Assessment opportunity
During the plenary, use the interactive activity 'Fantasy characters' to identify the characteristics of different characters. Then ask children to share their descriptions of their fantasy characters with the rest of the class. Assess how well they elaborate on their basic ideas. Children working at levels 2–3 can consider their word choices. Children working at levels 4-5 can discuss their characters in more detail and explain how they have attempted to create interest. Ask children probing questions such as: *Are your characters human? Do they have particular skills or magical traits? Do they have any particular fears or flaws? Do they have a weakness? Where do they live? What do they feed on? How will they behave? What will they say?* Afterwards, gather the activity sheets up and read through them all.

Assessment evidence
At levels 2–3, children's verbal responses and character sketches will include simple but mostly appropriate vocabulary. At levels 4–5, children's verbal responses will incorporate a more extensive range of vocabulary that suits each character role, for example, use of adverbs to describe actions. The completed photocopiable pages and children's verbal responses will provide evidence towards Writing AF7.

Next steps
Support: The children can draw pictures of each of their fantasy characters. Have them decorate the drawing of each character to match their roles. Ask them: *What will your villain wear/look like?* Encourage the children to use their drawings to help them to write their character sketches.
Extension: Invite children to come up with phrases or sentences to describe what the characters would do or say in different situations.

Key aspects of learning
Reasoning: Children will discuss the influence of settings on characters, using evidence from the text to justify their opinions and referring to wider evidence from their own knowledge and experience.
Communication: Children will often work collaboratively in pairs and groups. They will communicate outcomes orally, in writing and using other modes and media where appropriate.

NARRATIVE

Phase ② Planning a fantasy story

Learning outcome
Children can plan a story using the organisational features of the text type.

Success criteria
● I can use a story skeleton to plan my own fantasy story.
● I can decide what will be included in each paragraph to represent different events.

Setting the context
The children will have previously explored narrative structure and have prepared their own ideas for fantasy settings and characters. Model how to complete a story plan using photocopiable page 'Fantasy story plan', highlighting the four different stages of the story (introduction, build-up, climax and ending/resolution) and emphasising that each section, in this case the 'build-up', could have more than one paragraph. Ensure that children know that they should write in note form and not full sentences. Explain that their fantasy guide (who could also be the hero) will need to have a reason for their quest: to find a lost relative; to recover hidden treasure. Explain that along the way the guide will need to encounter danger during the climax of the story to create interest and tension for the reader.

Assessment opportunity
Allow time for all the children to make notes on the photocopiable page 'Fantasy story plan'. They can work in pairs or small groups to write ideas for each paragraph of the story. Encourage the children to orally retell their stories and check that their ideas make sense. Observe whether they incorporate descriptive detail and use linking devices such as time connectives. Once the children have finished their notes, bring the class back together and incorporate their imaginative ideas into a shared story plan. Ask the class the following questions in order to assess the success of the shared plan: *Is there a clear reason for the journey or quest? Have you included imaginative ideas for settings? Have you thought out the personality traits of the characters? This is a two-world story so have you included a trigger for moving from one world to the other? Are there any magical objects in the story and how do they fit in? What danger will your character encounter and how will they overcome this?* Encourage children to evaluate the shared writing against the success criteria and note their responses. Mark children's story plans according to the relevance of their ideas and how they elaborate on them.

Assessment evidence
At levels 2–3, children's verbal responses and story plans will mostly include ideas that are relevant to their story. Character and setting names may be accompanied by simple adjectives, for example, 'bad villain'. At levels 4–5, children's verbal responses and story plans will include content that is developed and is relevant. Descriptions will be more detailed and will include use of noun phrases and adverbial phrases. The children's marked story plans and verbal responses will provide evidence towards Writing AF1.

Next steps
Support: Devise a simplified fantasy story plan (three paragraphs) collaboratively, with an adult scribing the children's ideas and noting how they respond to leading questions.
Extension: Encourage children to think about the organisation of the stories and to detail cohesive devices that they will use to link the different paragraphs and stages of the story. Assess their ability to refine and extend their story plans with a clear beginning, a series of problems or obstacles, a climax and a final resolution.

Key aspects of learning
Evaluation: Children will discuss the success criteria they have devised to evaluate their own written work and give feedback to others.
Communication: Children will often work collaboratively in pairs and groups. They will communicate outcomes orally, in writing and using other modes and media where appropriate.

Phase ② Building tension

Learning outcome
Children can plan a story using the organisational features of the text type.

Success criteria
I can plan how to build up tension in my fantasy story.

Setting the context
The children will have previously explored narrative structure and they will also need to have prepared their own ideas for fantasy settings and characters. Read examples of how an author builds tension to the whole class, for example, when Twig meets the Gloamglozer on pages 260–264 of *Beyond the Deepwoods*. Point out that the author does not simply allow the fantasy guide to confront the fantasy villain but builds tension by describing the setting, providing the guide's knowledge of the villain, and describing what the guide hears, smells or feels before the encounter takes place. Tell the children they are going to plan a paragraph of tension-building before they begin writing their own fantasy stories.

Assessment opportunity
All children can work independently to complete the photocopiable page 'Building tension'. They should describe the setting in such a way as to build up a sensation of fear; they should describe the sounds and smells of the villain as well as the guide's prior knowledge of the villain to build the sensation before the actual meeting. Assess children's vocabulary choices and the appropriateness of the language that they have employed to build tension.

Assessment evidence
At levels 2–3, children will include simple but mostly appropriate vocabulary with some adventurous language used. At levels 4–5, children will include a wider range of vocabulary that has sometimes been chosen for effect. This activity will provide evidence towards Writing AF7.

Next steps
Support: Discuss situations in which the children have been nervous or scared and ask them to consider how their bodies react to the situation. Do their palms sweat? Does their stomach grind and grumble? Do the hairs on the back of their necks stand on end? Does their throat feel dry? Does their heart pound? Drawing on their own experiences will assist children with an imaginary situation.
Extension: Encourage children to incorporate similes and metaphors into their descriptions.

Key aspects of learning
Communication: Children will often work collaboratively in pairs and groups. They will communicate outcomes orally, in writing and using other modes and media where appropriate.

NARRATIVE

Phase ③ Writing a fantasy story

Learning outcome
Children can write a narrative using paragraphs to organise ideas maintaining cohesion within and between paragraphs.

Success criteria
● I can write a fantasy story using separate paragraphs for each stage of my story.
● I can use cohesive devices to link my paragraphs.
● I can use a review chart to make sure I have included all the features of a fantasy story.

Setting the context
Children will require plenty of time for this extended writing activity. They will need to refer to their setting photos, character planning sheets, tension-building notes and story plans from the previous activities in Phase 2. Before writing, ask the children to work in pairs and to tell their planned story to their talk partner. This will help to consolidate their ideas and allow feedback. Review the success criteria with the children and provide the photocopiable page 'Fantasy review' for them to use as a prompt during the oral telling of their stories and the writing process.

Assessment opportunity
Assess whether children can write independently using paragraphs to distinguish different stages of the story as well as their ability to create imaginative characters and settings. Check whether they have made the characters react to the setting and used dialogue and descriptions of their actions to show how they are feeling. Assess how they use cohesive devices to link the ideas between each paragraph – have they used effective connectives? Observe how well children use the 'Fantasy review' chart to ensure they have incorporated several key features of fantasy stories. Mark children's work against the success criteria listed above.

Assessment evidence
The children's fantasy stories will provide evidence for how well they can construct paragraphs in a piece of extended writing. At levels 2–3, children's stories will be loosely structured and may be written in one-sentence paragraphs. Some links between paragraphs using pronouns may also be evident. At levels 4–5, children's writing will be more clearly structured in extended paragraphs that link together in a mostly logical way. They may also link the paragraphs by using connectives. This activity should provide evidence towards Writing AF4.

Next steps
Support: Have the children write one story paragraph, focusing on one particular aspect of the story, for example, the opening paragraph where the setting and guide character are described and introduced.
Extension: Identify areas of the children's finished stories that require development, such as varying sentence structure, use of different sentence openers and the incorporation of effective descriptive language. Assist children with the editing process.

Key aspects of learning
Evaluation: Children will discuss the success criteria they have devised to evaluate their own written work and give feedback to others.
Communication: Children will often work collaboratively in pairs and groups. They will communicate outcomes orally, in writing and using other modes and media where appropriate.

Periodic assessment

Reading

Learning outcome Children can express opinions about an author's intended impact on a reader.	**Success criteria** I can explain how the author creates a fantasy setting with mood and atmosphere.

Setting the context Introduce the class to the story extract, *The Hobbit,* on the photocopiable page 'Narrative 2 Reading assessment text'. Explain that in the first two paragraphs of the extract, the reader is introduced to the world of the hobbit. The fantasy setting has many familiar features from the real world which the reader can identify with, and the description of the hobbit's home (the hole in The Hill) creates a warm, cosy, safe feeling. (This sense of security is very important to the story as it contrasts starkly with the journey on which Bilbo (the fantasy guide) later embarks.) The remaining paragraphs give a description of the guide character Bilbo with examples of hobbit species' characteristics (hobbits are humble, unadventurous and very home-loving). Read the whole story extract to the class.

Assessment opportunity Give each of the children the photocopiable pages 'Narrative 2 Reading assessment text' and 'Narrative 2 Reading assessment'. Ask them to read the text extract from *The Hobbit* and then to draw two detailed pictures of the story setting (The hobbit's home and The Hill). They will then draw a third picture of a hobbit. Following this the children will use words and phrases from the text to help them to create descriptive labels to annotate all of their pictures. Ask the children how the descriptions of the setting and guide character make them feel and make notes to capture their responses.

Assessment evidence At levels 2-3, children will identify effective words and phrases used by the author with little or no comment about the impact on the reader. At levels 4-5, children will be able to express what the descriptions make them think and feel. They will explain what impact they think the author wanted to create with his description, and discuss why they think this may be. The completed annotated drawings will provide evidence against Reading AF5. Use this activity and examples of children's work throughout this unit to make level judgements for Reading. |

Periodic assessment

NARRATIVE

Writing

Learning outcomes
Children can write a description of a fantasy setting which will create mood and atmosphere, using elements of the real world to hook the reader. Children can describe a fantasy guide and create an image in the reader's mind.

Success criteria
● I can describe a fantasy setting in detail, using strong adjectives and similes to help to create a mood.
● I can describe a fantasy guide character in detail.

Setting the context
The children need to have had prior knowledge of the features of the fantasy story text type. They can refer to their annotated drawings of *The Hobbit* setting (see the activity above) for ideas. Children will write descriptions of a fantasy setting and then a fantasy guide, in two introductory paragraphs in the style of JRR Tolkien. Explain that you want them to create an atmosphere of safety and warmth – the reader should want to go to their fantasy setting to meet their character and to explore their fantasy world. Explain that they must create a mood/atmosphere of safety in their description of the setting. Children should describe their fantasy guide both physically and in terms of personality traits which would be of relevance later in their stories.

Assessment opportunity
Hand out the photocopiable page 'Narrative 2 Writing assessment' and ask the children to write the two story paragraphs independently. Assess the children's vocabulary choices and the impact their descriptions have on you as a reader. Can children picture the setting they are creating before they try to write about it? Once they have an image in their heads, can they choose words carefully to let their readers into this world too? Can they use similes to create a greater impact? Can they determine a viewpoint which they wish the reader to adopt and can they describe how they have gone about achieving this? How are they going to make the reader feel that they would like to visit this place? How do they want the reader to feel about their fantasy character? If they want him or her to be comical, what features or traits will he or she have?

Assessment evidence
At levels 2–3, children's ideas will be mostly relevant with some nouns expanded by use of simple adjectives, for example, 'green door'. They may also demonstrate some attempt to adopt a particular viewpoint in their writing. Their choice of vocabulary will usually be simplistic with some words chosen for effect. At levels 4–5, children will develop their ideas in order to create an impact, for example, use of expanded nouns and adverbial phrases such as: 'the white, lace curtain fluttered gently' to describe the setting. They will establish and sustain a viewpoint in their writing. This activity will provide evidence against Writing AF1 and AF7. Use this activity and examples of children's work throughout the unit to make a level judgements for Writing.

SCHOLASTIC

Features of a fantasy story

Fantasy~world settings
Has features from the real world which have been twisted to make them strange.

Typical characters
Fantasy stories often contain a guide, helpers, a hero, and a villain.

Fantasy creatures often feature characteristics of real-world beings.

Triggers
An object that moves the guide between the real and fantasy worlds.

Quest or Journey
Often the guide will have to overcome evil or return something to its rightful owner.

Cliffhangers
A technique used by fantasy writers to create suspense and anticipation, spurring the reader on.

FANTASY WORLDS

Real~world Settings
A setting that will be familiar and instantly recognisable.

Problem & Resolution
In fantasy stories, there is often a battle of good over evil and a showdown between the hero and the villain.

Fantasy objects
There is often an object that has special magical powers – good or evil.

Illustration © 2001, Maggie Beard (2001, Scholastic).

NARRATIVE

UNIT 3 Stories from other cultures

Literacy objectives

Speak and listen for a wide range of purposes in different contexts
Strand 1 Speaking
- Use and reflect on some ground rules for sustaining talk and interactions.

Strand 2 Listening and responding
- Identify how talk varies with age, familiarity, gender and purpose.

Strand 4 Drama
- Create roles showing how behaviour can be interpreted from different viewpoints.

Read and write for a range of purposes on paper and on screen
Strand 7 Understanding and interpreting texts
- Identify and summarise evidence from a text to support a hypothesis.
- Deduce characters' reasons for behaviour from their actions and explain how ideas are developed in non-fiction texts.
- Explain how writers use figurative and expressive language to create images and atmosphere.

Strand 8 Engaging with and responding to texts
- Read extensively favourite authors or genres and experiment with other types of text.
- Interrogate texts to deepen and clarify understanding and response.

Strand 10 Text structure and organisation
- Organise text into paragraphs to distinguish between different information, events or processes.

Key aspects of learning

Communication
- Make connections and see relationships.

Managing feelings
- Recognise, label and think about feelings.

Empathy
- Recognise similarities and differences between themselves and others.

Motivation
- Carry out an activity to achieve an anticipated outcome. Take an interest in, watch and listen to other people.

Problem solving
- Look at and think about things differently and from other points of view.

Evaluation
- Express own views, opinions and preferences.

SCHOLASTIC

Assessment focuses

Reading
AF2 *(understand, describe, select or retrieve information, events or ideas from texts and use quotation and reference to text).*
AF3 *(deduce, infer or interpret information, events or ideas from texts).*
AF7 *(relate texts to their social, cultural, and historical contexts and literary traditions).*

Writing
AF1 *(write imaginative, interesting and thoughtful texts).*
AF4 *(construct paragraphs and use cohesion within and between paragraphs).*
AF6 *(write with technical accuracy of syntax and punctuation in phrases, clauses and sentences).*
AF8 *(use correct spelling).*

Speaking and listening
Speaking (use standard English appropriately).
Listening and responding (ask relevant questions and respond appropriately).
Drama (improvise and sustain roles).

Resources

Phase 1 activities
Gregory Cool by Caroline Binch (ISBN 978-0711-20890-2)
Photocopiable page, 'Comparison chart'
Interactive activity, 'Spidergram'
Access to Tobago websites such as www.mytobago.com
Photocopiable pages, 'Come to Tobago!' (versions 1 and 2)
Interactive activity, 'Come to Tobago!'
Phase 2 activities
Photocopiable pages, 'Gregory's holiday photographs' (versions 1 and 2)
Gregory Cool by Caroline Binch (ISBN 978-0711-20890-2)
Photocopiable page, 'Gregory's diary – day 3'
Phase 3 activities
Photocopiable page, 'Asking questions'
Periodic assessment
Photocopiable page, 'Narrative 3: Reading assessment text (a)'
Photocopiable page, 'Narrative 3 Reading assessment text (b)'
Photocopiable page, 'Narrative 3 Reading assessment'

Unit 3 ▢ Stories from other cultures

Learning outcomes	Assessment opportunity and evidence	Assessment focuses (AFs)		Success criteria
		Level 2	Level 3	
Phase ① activities pages 44–45				
Another culture Children can read stories from other cultures.	● Whole-class brainstorming activity where children recap cultural features of Tobago. ● Independent activity where children compare cultural features of Tobago with their home country. ● Completed whole-class spidergram; photocopiable pages.	**Reading AF7** ● General features of a few text types identified. ● Some awareness that books are set in different times and places.	**Reading AF7** ● Some simple connections between texts identified. ● Recognition of some features of the context of texts.	● I can identify details from a text which tell me that a story is from another culture. ● I compare my life with that of the characters' lives in a story.
Where is Tobago? Children can find facts about the country in which a story is set.	● Paired activity where children use the internet to find out specific facts about Tobago. ● Completed photocopiable pages.	**Reading AF2** ● Some specific, straightforward information recalled. ● Generally clear idea of where to look for information.	**Reading AF2** ● Simple, most obvious points identified though there may also be some misunderstanding. ● Some comments include quotations from or references to text, but not always relevant.	I can use research to find facts about a country.
Phase ② activities pages 45–47				
How characters behave Children can discuss characters and predict how settings have an impact on behaviour.	● Supported group activity where children infer how a character, Gregory, will behave based on evidence from the text. ● Completed photocopiable pages; children's oral responses.	**Reading AF3** ● Simple, plausible inference about events and information, using evidence from text. ● Comments based on textual cues, sometimes misunderstood.	**Reading AF3** ● Straightforward inference based on a single point of reference in the text. ● Responses to text show meaning established at a literal level.	I can give reasons for a character's behaviour using evidence from the text.
How are they feeling? Children know how a story is organised through paragraphs and connectives. Children can predict how a story setting will affect a character's behaviour.	● Independent activity where children write diary entries in the first person. ● Completed diary entries.	**Writing AF4** Ideas in sections grouped by content, some linking by simple pronouns.	**Writing AF4** ● Some internal structure within sections of text. ● Within paragraphs/ sections, some links between sentences. ● Movement between paragraphs/sections sometimes abrupt or disjointed.	● I can write a diary entry in the first person. ● I can use paragraphs to separate different events. ● I can use time connectives to place events in order.
Phase ③ activities pages 47–48				
Asking questions Children can devise and ask questions using informal language.	● Independent activity where children devise questions to ask Gregory from *Gregory Cool*. ● Whole-class discussion and hot-seating activity. Completed photocopiable pages; children's oral responses.	**Writing AF6** ● Clause structure mostly grammatically correct. ● Sentence demarcation with capital letters and full stops usually accurate. ● Some accurate use of question and exclamation marks, and commas in lists.	**Writing AF6** ● Straightforward sentences usually demarcated accurately with full stops, capital letters, question and exclamation marks. ● Some, limited, use of speech punctuation. ● Comma splicing evident, particularly in narrative.	● I can write and ask open questions to find out more about a character. ● I can explain how formal and informal speech varies.

Unit 3 ◻ Stories from other cultures

Learning outcomes	Assessment opportunity and evidence	Assessment focuses (AFs)		Success criteria
		Level 4	Level 5	

Phase ① activities pages 44–45

Learning outcomes	Assessment opportunity and evidence	Level 4	Level 5	Success criteria
Another culture Children can read stories from other cultures.	● Whole-class brainstorming activity where children recap cultural features of Tobago. ● Independent activity where children compare cultural features of Tobago with their home country. ● Completed whole-class spidergram; photocopiable pages.	**Reading AF7** ● Features common to different texts or versions of the same text identified, with simple comment. ● Simple comment on the effect that the reader's or writer's context has on the meaning of texts.	**Reading AF7** ● Comments identify similarities and differences between texts, or versions, with some explanation. ● Some explanation of how the contexts in which texts are written and read contribute to meaning.	● I can identify details from a text which tell me that a story is from another culture. ● I can compare my life with that of the characters' lives in a story.
Where is Tobago? Children can find facts about the country in which a story is set.	● Paired activity where children use the internet to find out specific facts about Tobago. ● Children write up their research using conditional sentences. ● Completed photocopiable pages.	**Reading AF2** ● Some relevant points identified. ● Comments supported by some generally relevant textual reference or quotation.	**Reading AF2** ● Most relevant points clearly identified, including those selected from different places in the text. ● Comments generally supported by relevant textual reference or quotation, even when points made are not always accurate.	I can use research to find facts about a country.

Phase ② activities pages 45–47

Learning outcomes	Assessment opportunity and evidence	Level 4	Level 5	Success criteria
How characters behave Children can discuss characters and predict how settings have an impact on behaviour.	● Supported group activity where children infer how a character, Gregory, will behave based on evidence from the text. ● Completed photocopiable pages; children's oral responses.	**Reading AF3** ● Comments make inference based on evidence from different points in the text. ● Inferences often correct, but comments are not always rooted securely in the text or repeat narrative content.	**Reading AF3** ● Comments develop explanation of inferred meanings drawing on evidence across the text. ● Comments make inferences and deductions based on textual evidence.	I can give reasons for a character's behaviour using evidence from the text.
How are they feeling? Children know how a story is organised through paragraphs and connectives. Children can predict how a story setting will affect a character's behaviour.	● Independent activity where children write diary entries in the first person. ● Completed diary entries.	**Writing AF4** ● Paragraphs/sections help to organise content. ● Within paragraphs/ sections, limited range of connections between sentences. ● Some attempts to establish simple links between paragraphs/ sections not always maintained.	**Writing AF4** ● Paragraphs clearly structure main ideas across text to support purpose. ● Within paragraphs/ sections, a range of devices support cohesion. ● Links between paragraphs/ sections generally maintained across whole text.	● I can write a diary entry in the first person. ● I can use paragraphs to separate different events. ● I can use time connectives to place events in order.

Phase ③ activities pages 47–48

Learning outcomes	Assessment opportunity and evidence	Level 4	Level 5	Success criteria
Asking questions Children can devise and ask questions using informal language.	● Independent activity where children devise questions to ask Gregory from *Gregory Cool*. ● Whole-class discussion and hot-seating activity. ● Completed photocopiable pages; children's oral responses.	**Writing AF6** ● Sentences demarcated accurately throughout the text, including question marks. ● Speech marks to denote speech generally accurate, with some other speech punctuation.	**Writing AF6** ● Full range of punctuation used accurately to demarcate sentences, including speech punctuation. ● Syntax and punctuation within the sentence generally accurate including commas to mark clauses, though some errors occur where ambitious structures are attempted.	● I can write and ask open questions to find out more about a character. ● I can recognise how formal and informal speech varies.

NARRATIVE

Phase ① Another culture

Learning outcome
Children can read stories from other cultures.

Success criteria
- I can identify details from a text which tell me that a story is from another culture.
- I can compare my life with that of the characters' lives in a story.

Setting the context
Gregory Cool is the story of a young boy from London who goes on holiday to visit his grandparents and cousin, Lennox, in Tobago. Gregory finds the country and its cultural differences difficult to adjust to at first but after a few days he begins to change his mind. Read the story with the whole class, asking them to listen for and to identify features in the story which indicate that it is from another place and culture.

Assessment opportunity
After the shared reading of the story, ask the children to identify features which indicate that the story is from a different place and culture. Prompt responses by asking questions such as: *What was the weather like? What was his grandparents' house like? Describe the food that Gregory tried. What was different about the beaches? What could they hear at night-time that was different to the UK? What animals did Gregory encounter that he would not have seen in everyday life in the UK?* Use the interactive activity 'Spidergram' to brainstorm the cultural features of Tobago. Then give the children the photocopiable page 'Comparison chart' to make a note of all the cultural differences between Tobago and their home country. Encourage them to make comparisons between the culture that Gregory encounters and their own personal experiences. Challenge children working at levels 4–5 to think of other stories they have read that are set in other countries. Observe and record children's verbal responses.

Assessment evidence
At levels 2–3, children will show some awareness that the story is from another culture. At levels 4–5, children will be able to draw comparisons with other stories they have read from different cultures. The children's verbal responses and annotations will provide evidence against Reading AF7 (see also Reading AF2).

Next steps
Support: Re-read the text again as a guided group, stopping after small chunks of text. Identify and collate cultural features as you progress through the story rather than at the end.
Extension: Encourage children to make predictions about other differences between the two cultures. For example, what differences do they think there may be between Gregory and Lennox's schools?

Key aspects of learning
Communication: Make connections and see relationships.
Empathy: Recognise similarities and differences between themselves and others.

Phase ① Where is Tobago?

Learning outcome
Children can find facts about the country in which a story is set.

Success criteria
I can use research to find facts about a country.

Setting the context
This activity assumes that children have read the story *Gregory Cool*. Ask children which country Gregory went to visit (Tobago). Locate Tobago on a world map and on a globe. Discuss its location in relation to the equator. Discuss which waters surround Tobago. Discuss which countries and oceans Gregory would have flown over in order to arrive there.

Assessment opportunity
Divide the children into pairs and provide them with access to a suitable website (eg www.justtobago.co.uk) to enable them to carry out research about Tobago. Children working at levels 2-3 can use version 1 of the photocopiable page 'Come to Tobago!' to guide their research. Assess whether they can retrieve relevant information from the website. Can they select the information that they need and disregard the rest? Children working at levels 4-5 can complete version 2 of the photocopiable page following their internet research. They can write conditional sentences that describe what a tourist could do if they visited Tobago. Encourage children to retrieve descriptive language from the website to paint a vivid picture of Tobago.

Assessment evidence
At levels 2-3, children will retrieve simple information such as names of places and wildlife. At levels 4-5, children's written response will be supported by appropriate quotations from the website. The completed activity will provide evidence against Reading AF2.

Next steps
Support: Have the children use a prepared simplified text to practise retrieval of information.
Extension: Have the children use the interactive activity 'Come to Tobago!' to further extend their research skills. Alternatively, ask them to create a tourist pamphlet about Tobago, using paragraphs to separate different ideas and using persuasive language to entice the reader.

Key aspects of learning
Motivation: Carry out an activity to achieve an anticipated outcome.

Phase ② How characters behave

Learning outcome
Children can discuss characters and predict how settings have an impact on behaviour.

Success criteria
I can give reasons for a character's behaviour using evidence from the text.

Setting the context
Re-read the story *Gregory Cool* with the whole class. Discuss how Gregory's feelings changed over time. Why do the children think this was? Draw out suggestions from the children that the differences in lifestyle between his home in England and his family's home in Tobago made Gregory uneasy at first and he was dismissive. But once Gregory got used to his surroundings, he relaxed and enjoyed himself. Encourage the children to back up their comments with evidence from the text.

Unit 3 ▢ Stories from other cultures

▷ Assessment opportunity

After shared reading of the story, all the children can work in supported discussion groups to use the photocopiable page 'Gregory's holiday photographs (version 1 or 2)'. Ask the children to look at the images on the photocopiable page to remind them of the story. Ask them to suggest two photographs that they think Gregory would take and to give reasons as to why he would have taken them. Support the children when they are recording their ideas. Ask them: *Why do you think Gregory would take these photographs? What was he feeling at the time? How do you know he was feeling this way?* Extend children working at levels 2-3 by asking questions such as: *How had Gregory's feelings changed? And how had the setting influenced his feelings? How do you know?* Encourage the children to refer back to the text to support their inferences. Record the children's responses to the questions.

Assessment evidence

At levels 2-3, children's verbal responses will provide evidence of their ability to make basic inferences using information from the text. At levels 4-5, children will be able to empathise with characters in a story. Their comments will make inferences about characters' behaviour based on evidence from the different points in the text. They will draw conclusions about Gregory's behaviour and his feelings. This activity will provide evidence towards Reading AF3.

Next steps

Support: In a guided reading group, use a different story from another culture to practise the skills of inference and deduction with the children. Encourage them to refer back to illustrations as well as the text to provide evidence for their comments.
Extension: During a group reading session, invite children to recall other situations in stories they have read where a character's behaviour is influenced by the setting. Ask them to locate the books and find the examples. For each example, ask the children: *How did the setting affect the character's behaviour? How were they feeling? How do you know? What did the character do? Why do you think the character did this?* Encourage them to back up their deductions by referring to the character's dialogue as well as their actions.

▢ Key aspects of learning

Communication: Make connections and see relationships.

Phase ② How are they feeling?

Learning outcomes

Children know how a story is organised through paragraphs and connectives. Children can predict how a story setting will affect a character's behaviour.

Success criteria
- I can write a diary entry in the first person.
- I can use paragraphs to separate different events.
- I can use time connectives to place events in order.

Setting the context

This activity assumes that children have read and discussed the story *Gregory Cool*. They will also need to have prior knowledge of structuring and organising narrative texts. Re-read the story, to the children, from the morning of Gregory's third day on Tobago. Explain that the story is written in the third person, and that Gregory's feelings are evident from the author's descriptions of his behaviour. Compare the original story to the diary entry on the photocopiable page 'Gregory's diary - day 3' to show how the text has changed from the third to the first person. Explain to the children that diary entry is incomplete and that they should continue writing the diary entry from Gregory's point of view, in the first person. Review the success criteria and display it for the children to refer to during the activity.

Assessment opportunity

Ask the children to read the diary entry on the photocopiable page 'Gregory's diary – day 3' and then to independently complete the writing of the diary entry in the first person. Note: the children are likely to need additional sheets of paper to complete their diary entries. Observe whether the children reflect Gregory's feelings in their diary entries. Ask prompt questions such as: *How is Gregory feeling at the end of the day? What does he do that tells you he is more at ease now?* Assess whether children have organised their ideas into paragraphs and whether they have linked paragraphs through use of cohesive devices such as connectives. Assess children's ability to sustain the writing form, ie in the first person using the past tense. Have they consistently used the correct verb form? Have they maintained the style of a diary entry? Does the content of their writing reflect an understanding of the character's feelings and how the setting has influenced him? Encourage children to group their ideas into clearly demarcated paragraphs.

Assessment evidence

At levels 2–3, children will organise their ideas loosely and may write in single-sentence paragraphs. They may sometimes use simple time connectives to link the sections of their diary entry. At levels 4–5, children will organise their content more clearly with writing organised into longer paragraphs. This activity will provide evidence towards mainly Writing AF4 (see also Writing AF6).

Next steps

Support: For children who have difficulty writing in the first person, provide them with a simple third-person sentence made up of individual word cards, for example, 'She went to school'. Work with them to identify the pronoun in the sentence and to exchange this word card for a first person pronoun (I, we). Then ask them to check whether changes need to be made to the verb in the sentence. Repeat the activity with different sentences.

Extension: Ask the children to imagine that they are Gregory. They should write a letter to their parents, summarising the first three days of their trip. Encourage them to explain what they have experienced, how it felt to them at the time and how their feelings have changed.

Key aspects of learning

Communication: Make connections and see relationships.
Managing feelings: Recognise, label and think about feelings.
Empathy: Recognise similarities and differences between themselves and others.

Phase ③ Asking questions

Learning outcome
Children can devise and ask questions using informal language.

Success criteria
● I can write and ask open questions to find out more about a character.
● I can explain how formal and informal speech varies.

Setting the context

This activity assumes that the children have read the story *Gregory Cool*. Select a volunteer to be Gregory. Explain to the whole class that they should imagine they are in Gregory's class in England and that they are going to interview Gregory on his return about his trip to Tobago. Ask the children to write open questions to ask Gregory (recap how to write a question that will not result in a yes/no response). Discuss whether the language used during questioning should be formal or informal and demonstrate examples of each.

Assessment opportunity

All the children can use the photocopiable page 'Asking questions'. Once children have written their questions, carry out a hot-seating activity with a volunteer

NARRATIVE

playing the role of Gregory. Then repeat this activity but with the children imagining that they are now newspaper reporters doing an interview with Gregory about his journey to Tobago. Discuss how the questions would vary and how different people would ask questions from a different point of view. Give the children time to translate their questions into more formal language. Assess the children's ability to correctly structure and punctuate questions.

Assessment evidence
At levels 2–3, children will punctuate most sentences correctly including the use of a capital letter and a question mark. The grammatical structure of straightforward sentences should usually be correct. At levels 4–5, all sentences should be punctuated correctly and grammar should also be mostly accurate. This activity will provide evidence towards Writing AF6 (see also Writing AF8).

Next steps
Support: For children who have difficulty in devising questions, provide a specific topic on which to base questions, such as asking Gregory a question about swimming in the sea.
Extension: Have the children 'hot-seat' different characters from the story, such as Gregory's cousin, his grandparents or the fishermen.

Key aspects of learning
Communication: Make connections and see relationships.
Managing feelings: Recognise, label and think about feelings.
Motivation: Carry out an activity to achieve an anticipated outcome. Take an interest in, watch and listen to other people.
Problem solving: Look at and think about things differently and from other points of view.

Periodic assessment

Reading

Learning outcomes
Children can read stories from other cultures.
Children can discuss characters and predict how settings have an impact on behaviour.

Success criteria
I can identify how settings have an impact on behaviour.

Setting the context
Explain to the class that they are going to read the start of a story about a girl who is going to Malaysia to meet her grandparents for the first time. They are then going to read a fact file about Penang, an island and province of northeast Malaysia, to learn about the culture of the Malaysian people.

Assessment opportunity
Hand out the photocopiable pages 'Narrative 3 Reading assessment text (a)' and 'Narrative 3 Reading assessment text (b)'. Ask the children to read both extracts and to work independently to answer the questions on the photocopiable page 'Narrative 3 Reading assessment'. Assess how well children are able to source evidence from the texts and draw inferences.

Assessment evidence
At levels 2–3, children's responses will contain basic information from the texts. They will make simple inferences about events. At levels 4–5, children will support their comments with textual quotes. The children's answers will provide evidence against Reading AF2, AF3 and AF7. Use this activity and evidence gathered during this unit to judge children's overall level in Reading.

Writing

Learning outcomes
Children know how a story is organised through paragraphs and connectives.
Children can discuss characters and predict how settings have an impact on behaviour.

Success criteria
● I can write a new paragraph for each new idea.
● I can link my paragraphs using connectives.

Setting the context
This activity assumes that the children have carried out the activity above. Re-read the extract from the photocopiable page 'Narrative 3 Reading assessment text (a)'. Model how to write the next paragraph of the story, using facts from the photocopiable page 'Narrative 3 Reading assessment text (b)'. Brainstorm the experiences Amelina may have: trying new food, going to the beach, seeing new buildings and so on. Display the story extract and the success criteria for the children to refer to during the independent activity.

Assessment opportunity
After the shared writing, children can continue to write the story in several paragraphs. Children working at levels 2–3 may prefer to write one paragraph to describe a single event. Assess how well they draw on relevant information from the texts to construct their stories. Have they used one paragraph for one idea? Have they linked paragraphs cohesively?

Assessment evidence
The children's stories will provide evidence against Writing AF1, AF4 and AF6. Look for thoughtful and appropriate content, use of paragraphs, and accurate grammar and punctuation. Use the completed stories and examples of children's work gathered during this unit to assess overall levels in Writing.

NARRATIVE

Name _____ Date _____

Comparison chart

◀ Think about the differences between life in Tobago and the country where you live.

◀ List these differences in the chart below.

Your home country	Tobago

Illustration © Bill Houston/Bill Houston Creative Limited

Red
Amber
Green

I can identify details from a text which tell me that a story is from another culture. ⬚

I can compare my life with that of the characters' lives in a story. ⬚

Name	Date

Asking questions

Illustration © 1994 Caroline Binch.

I can write and ask open questions to find out more about a character. ☐

I can explain how formal and informal speech varies. ☐

NARRATIVE

UNIT 4 Stories which raise issues/dilemmas

Literacy objectives

Speak and listen for a wide range of purposes in different contexts

Strand 4 Drama
- Create roles showing how behaviour can be interpreted from different viewpoints.

Read and write for a range of purposes on paper and on screen

Strand 7 Understanding and interpreting texts
- Deduce characters' reasons for behaviour from their actions and explain how ideas are developed in non-fiction texts.

Strand 9 Creating and shaping texts
- Develop and refine ideas in writing using planning and problem-solving strategies.
- Use settings and characterisation to engage readers' interest.
- Show imagination through the language used to create emphasis, humour, atmosphere or suspense.

Strand 10 Text structure and organisation
- Organise text into paragraphs to distinguish between different information, events or processes.

Strand 11 Sentence structure and punctuation
- Clarify meaning and points of view by using varied sentence structure (phrases, clauses and adverbials).

Key aspects of learning

Empathy
- By taking part in role-play activities, children will be able to identify more closely with fictional characters and will be helped to understand their feelings and actions.

Communication
- Children will develop their ability to work collaboratively in pairs, groups or whole-class contexts. They will communicate outcomes orally, in writing and through use of ICT if appropriate.

Creative thinking
- Children will consider alternatives to story endings and will create a new ending of their own.

Social skills
- When working collaboratively, children will listen to and will respect other people's ideas. They will take on different roles in a group.

Reasoning
- Children will discuss the influence of issues on characters, using evidence from the text to justify their opinions and referring to wider evidence from their own knowledge and experience.

Self-awareness
- As they work on an extended piece of writing, children will learn how to organise their own work and how to maintain their concentration to complete a polished story.

Assessment focuses

Reading
AF2 (*understand, describe, select or retrieve information, events or ideas from texts and use quotation and reference to text*).
AF3 (*deduce, infer or interpret information, events or ideas from texts*).
AF6 (*identify and comment on writers' purposes and viewpoints, and the overall effect of the text on the reader*).

Writing
AF1 (*write imaginative, interesting and thoughtful texts*).
AF3 (*organise and present whole texts effectively, sequencing and structuring information, ideas and events*).
AF4 (*construct paragraphs and use cohesion within and between paragraphs*).

Speaking and listening
Drama (improvise and sustain roles; work with others in performance).

Resources

Phase 1 activities
Photocopiable page, 'Beat the Bully'
Photocopiable page, 'Story outline'
Interactive activity, 'Story outline'
Phase 2 activities
The Worry Website by Jacqueline Wilson (ISBN 978-0440-86826-2)
Photocopiable page, 'Holly's Worry'
Interactive activity, 'Holly's Worry – points of view'
Photocopiable page, 'Advice for Holly'
Phase 3 activities
Photocopiable page, 'Mr Speed's class'
Photocopiable page, 'Story planner'
Photocopiable page, 'Are you ready to write?'
Photocopiable page, 'My character's feelings and actions'
Photocopiable page, 'Editorial review'
Periodic assessment
Photocopiable page, 'Narrative 4 Reading assessment text'
Photocopiable page, 'Narrative 4 Reading assessment'
Photocopiable page, 'Narrative 4 Writing assessment'

Unit 4 ◻ Stories which raise issues/dilemmas

Learning outcomes	Assessment opportunity and evidence	Assessment focuses (AFs)		Success criteria
		Level 2	Level 3	
Phase ① activities pages 57-58				
Beat the bully Children can predict outcomes and explore possible courses of action. Children can write a story with a clear structure.	● Group drama activity where children role play potential outcomes for a story. ● Supported activity where children write the climax and the ending of a story. ● Self-evaluation. ● Teacher's notes.	**Writing AF1** ● Mostly relevant ideas and content, sometimes repetitive or sparse. ● Some apt word choices create interest. ● Brief comments, questions about events or actions suggest viewpoint.	**Writing AF1** ● Some appropriate ideas and content included. ● Some attempt to elaborate on basic information or events. ● Attempt to adopt viewpoint, though often not maintained or inconsistent.	● I can write my own story climax and ending. ● I can use paragraphs for each stage of my story. ● I can link my ending to the beginning of the story.
Summarise the story Children can identify and summarise issues and how characters deal with them.	● Independent activity where children use the interactive activity to sequence paragraphs to create a story outline. ● Completed interactive activity.	**Reading AF2** ● Some specific, straightforward information recalled. ● Generally clear idea of where to look for information.	**Reading AF2** ● Simple, most obvious points identified though there may also be some misunderstanding. ● Some comments include quotations from or references to text, but not always relevant.	I can summarise the key points in each paragraph to produce a story outline.
Phase ② activities pages 59-61				
Holly's worry Children can identify and discuss evidence that suggests the character's point of view.	● Whole-class activity where children identify examples of characters' points of view in a text extract from *The Worry Website*. ● Highlighted text extracts; children's oral contributions.	**Reading AF2** ● Some specific, straightforward information recalled. ● Generally clear idea of where to look for information.	**Reading AF2** ● Simple, most obvious points identified though there may also be some misunderstanding . ● Some comments include quotations from or references to text, but not always relevant.	I can find evidence in the text which suggests a character's point of view.
This is what I think… Children can discuss different characters' points of view.	● Group activity where children discuss the characters' points of view. ● Children's oral responses.	**Reading AF3** ● Simple, plausible inference about events and information, using evidence from text. ● Comments based on textual cues, sometimes misunderstood.	**Reading AF3** ● Straightforward inference based on a single point of reference in the text. ● Responses to text show meaning established at a literal level.	● I can explain how different characters feel about an issue. ● I can give reasons for a character's feelings.
My advice is… Children can write giving advice to the main character	● Independent activity where children write some advice for Holly. ● Peer-evaluation. ● Completed photocopiable pages.	**Writing AF1** ● Mostly relevant ideas and content, sometimes repetitive or sparse. ● Some apt word choices create interest. ● Brief comments, questions about events or actions suggest viewpoint.	**Writing AF1** ● Some appropriate ideas and content included. ● Some attempt to elaborate on basic information or events. ● Attempt to adopt viewpoint, though often not maintained or inconsistent.	● I can write a paragraph giving advice to a main character of a story. ● I can suggest sensible solutions for the character's problems. ● I can give reasons for my advice.
Phase ③ activities pages 61-63				
My Worry Website plan Children can use a setting, characters and issue/dilemma to plan a story.	● Independent activity where children complete a plan for a story with an issue/ dilemma. ● Children's completed story plans.	**Writing AF3** ● Some basic sequencing of ideas or material. ● Openings and/or closings sometimes signalled.	**Writing AF3** ● Some attempt to organise ideas with related points placed next to each other. ● Openings and closings usually signalled. ● Some attempt to sequence ideas or material logically.	● I can explore a problem/issue and develop it to create a structure for my story. ● I can plan my story using a story planner.

Unit 4 ◻ Stories which raise issues/dilemmas

Learning outcomes	Assessment opportunity and evidence	Assessment focuses (AFs)		Success criteria
		Level 2	Level 3	
My Worry Website story Children can write a longer story in paragraphs.	• Independent activity where children use a story plan to write a story about a dilemma. • Children's completed stories.	**Writing AF4** Ideas in sections grouped by content, some linking by simple pronouns.	**Writing AF4** • Some internal structure within sections of text. • Within paragraphs/ sections, some links between sentences. • Movement between paragraphs/sections sometimes abrupt or disjointed.	• I can write a story about a dilemma using paragraphs for each stage of the story. • I can show how the main character feels by describing his or her actions. • I can use dialogue in my story to develop the plot.
Editorial reviews Children can carry out peer assessment of each other's stories.	• Mixed-ability groups where children carry out peer assessment of a story using the success criteria. • Children's oral contributions; completed photocopiable pages.	**Reading AF6** • Some awareness that writers have viewpoints and purposes. • Simple statements about likes and dislikes in reading, sometimes with reasons.	**Reading AF6** • Comments identify main purpose. • Express personal response but with little awareness of writer's viewpoint or effect on reader.	• I can review stories written by my peers. • I can identify the dilemma in my peer's story. • I can make constructive comments to help others to improve their work.

Learning outcomes	Assessment opportunity and evidence	Assessment focuses (AFs)		Success criteria
		Level 4	Level 5	

Phase ① activities pages 57–58

Learning outcomes	Assessment opportunity and evidence	Level 4	Level 5	Success criteria
Beat the bully Children can predict outcomes and explore possible courses of action. Children can write a story with a clear structure.	• Group drama activity where children role play potential outcomes for a story. • Independent activity where children write a climax, resolution and ending of a story. • Self-evaluation. • Teacher's notes.	**Writing AF1** • Relevant ideas and content chosen. • Some ideas and material developed in detail. • Straightforward viewpoint generally established and maintained.	**Writing AF1** • Relevant ideas and material developed with some imaginative detail. • Development of ideas and material appropriately shaped for selected form. • Clear viewpoint established, generally consistent, with some elaboration.	• I can write my own story climax and ending. • I can use paragraphs for each stage of my story. • I can link my ending to the beginning of the story.
Summarise the story Children can identify and summarise issues and how characters deal with them.	• Independent activity where children create a story outline. by summarising the paragraphs of a story. • Annotated story extracts; completed photocopiable pages.	**Reading AF2** • Some relevant points identified. • Comments supported by some generally relevant textual reference or quotation.	**Reading AF2** • Most relevant points clearly identified, including those selected from different places in the text. • Comments generally supported by relevant textual reference or quotation, even when points made are not always accurate.	I can summarise the key points in each paragraph to produce a story outline.

Phase ② activities pages 59–61

Learning outcomes	Assessment opportunity and evidence	Level 4	Level 5	Success criteria
Holly's worry Children can identify and discuss evidence that suggests the character's point of view.	• Whole-class activity where children identify examples of characters' points of view in a text extract from *The Worry Website*. • Highlighted text extracts; children's oral contributions.	**Reading AF2** • Some relevant points identified. • Comments supported by some generally relevant textual reference or quotation.	**Reading AF2** • Most relevant points clearly identified, including those selected from different places in the text. • Comments generally supported by relevant textual reference or quotation, even when points made are not always accurate.	I can find evidence in the text which suggests a character's point of view.

Unit 4 ▢ Stories which raise issues/dilemmas

Learning outcomes	Assessment opportunity and evidence	Assessment focuses (AFs)		Success criteria
		Level 4	Level 5	
This is what I think… Children can discuss different characters' points of view.	• Group activity where children discuss the characters' points of view. • Children's oral responses.	**Reading AF3** • Comments make inferences based on evidence from different points in the text. • Inferences often correct, but comments are not always rooted securely in the text or repeat narrative or content.	**Reading AF3** • Comments develop explanation of inferred meanings drawing on evidence across the text . • Comments make inferences and deductions based on textual evidence.	• I can explain how different characters feel about an issue. • I can give reasons for a character's feelings.
My advice is… Children can write giving advice to the main character.	• Independent activity where children write some advice for Holly. • Peer-evaluation. • Completed photocopiable pages.	**Writing AF1** • Relevant ideas and content chosen • Some ideas and material developed in detail • Straightforward viewpoint generally established and maintained	**Writing AF1** • Relevant ideas and material developed with some imaginative detail • Development of ideas and material appropriately shaped for selected form • Clear viewpoint established, generally consistent, with some elaboration	• I can write a paragraph giving advice to a main character of a story. • I can suggest sensible solutions for the character's problems. • I can give reasons for my advice.

Phase ③ activities pages 61–63

Learning outcomes	Assessment opportunity and evidence	Level 4	Level 5	Success criteria
My Worry Website plan Children can use a setting, characters and issue/dilemma to plan a story.	• Independent activity where children complete a plan for a story with an issue/dilemma. • Children's completed story plans.	**Writing AF3** • Ideas organised by clustering related points or by time sequence. • Ideas are organised simply with a fitting opening and closing, sometimes linked. • Ideas or material generally in logical sequence but overall direction of writing not always clearly signalled.	**Writing AF3** • Material is structured clearly, with sentences organised into appropriate paragraphs. • Development of material is effectively managed across text. • Overall direction of the text supported by clear links between paragraphs.	• I can explore a problem/issue and develop it to create a structure for my story. • I can plan my story using a story planner.
My Worry Website story Children can write a longer story in paragraphs.	• Independent activity where children use a story plan to write a story about a dilemma. • Children's completed stories.	**Writing AF4** • Paragraphs/sections help to organise content. • Within paragraphs/sections, limited range of connections between sentences. • Some attempts to establish simple links between paragraphs/sections not always maintained.	**Writing AF4** • Paragraphs clearly structure main ideas across text to support purpose. • Within paragraphs/sections, a range of devices. support cohesion. • Links between paragraphs/sections generally maintained across whole text.	• I can write a story about a dilemma using paragraphs for each stage of the story. • I can show how the main character feels by describing his or her actions. • I can use dialogue in my story to develop the plot.
Editorial reviews Children can carry out peer assessment of each other's stories.	• Mixed-ability groups where children carry out peer assessment of a story using the success criteria. • Children's oral contributions; completed photocopiable pages.	**Reading AF6** • Main purpose identified. • Simple comments show some awareness of writer's viewpoint . • Simple comment on overall effect on reader.	**Reading AF6** • Main purpose clearly identified, often through general overview. • Viewpoint in texts clearly identified, with some, often limited, explanation. • General awareness of effect on the reader, with some, often limited, explanation.	• I can review stories written by my peers. • I can identify the dilemma in my peer's story. • I can make constructive comments to help others to improve their work.

Phase ① Beat the bully

Learning outcomes
Children can predict outcomes and explore possible courses of action. Children can write a story with a clear structure.

Success criteria
- I can write my own story climax and ending.
- I can use paragraphs for each stage of my story.
- I can link my ending to the beginning of the story.

Setting the context
The activity assumes that the children have had experience writing and organising narrative texts. Read the story extract from the photocopiable page, 'Beat the Bully' to the whole class, up until the end of the fourth paragraph. Explain that you have read the opening, the dilemma/issue, the build-up and the key action. The next three stages are the conflict, the resolution and the ending (which links back to the opening). Say to the children: *Tim is going to meet Billy on the way to school, but what will happen?*

Assessment opportunity
Divide the children into groups of four. Ask them to discuss potential outcomes and to use members of the group to create a freeze-frame of Billy and Tim. The remaining two members of the group should suggest body positions and gestures for the pair. Observe how well children develop their ideas during the drama activity. Then ask all the children to write the last two paragraphs of the story (the climax and the ending). Share the success criteria with the children so they can refer to it throughout the activity. Children working at levels 2-3 can write with adult support. Assess their ability to structure the ideas into two paragraphs, to expand descriptions of characters with adjectives and to include relevant information. At levels 4-5, children can work independently to complete the story. Invite these children to consider how they can use Tim's interest in nature (fascination with insects), and his personality (his intelligence) to create a resolution. Can children tie the start of the story in with the ending? Do they think realistically about the likely behaviour of the main character? Have they used dialogue effectively? Ask the children to use the success criteria to evaluate their work.

Assessment evidence
At levels 2-3, children's writing will include some appropriate information with a few descriptive words used to add interest. At levels 4-5, children's writing will be more imaginative and they will produce a realistic climax and an ending that reflects their knowledge of the main character from the information given. They will also tie in the ending to the start of the story. This activity will provide evidence towards mainly Writing AF1 (see also Writing AF3 and Writing AF4).

Next steps
Support: If children find it difficult developing their ideas and considering possible actions, create a bank of cards with possible outcomes for them to consider. They may then choose their ending and develop it from this point. The children can work in groups with an adult scribe assisting them with modelling their ideas into sentences.
Extension: Children can write an alternative story or ending from the point of view of Billy the Bully. Can they consider why he behaved as he did? How do they think he was really feeling?

Key aspects of learning
Empathy: By taking part in role-play activities, children will be able to identify more closely with fictional characters and will be helped to understand their feelings and actions.
Creative thinking: Children will use creative thinking to consider alternatives to story endings and create a new ending of their own.
Social skills: When working collaboratively, children will listen to and respect other people's ideas. They will take on different roles in a group.

NARRATIVE

Phase ① Summarise the story

Learning outcome
Children can identify and summarise issues and how characters deal with them.

Success criteria
I can summarise the key points in each paragraph to produce a story outline.

Setting the context
Read the whole story extract from the photocopiable page 'Beat the Bully'. Revise the stages in a story, using the photocopiable page 'Story outline' and then recap on the definition of a paragraph, explaining that it represents a series of one or more sentences which are all about one idea. Select children to number some of the paragraphs in the story and then together decide which stage of the story each paragraph represents. If needed, help the children by telling them that there are seven paragraphs in the extract. Point out that dialogue should be considered as part of the previous paragraph. Discuss what is meant by key points and summary and help children to highlight the key words/phrases in the first paragraph and then to summarise the paragraph using the key words highlighted.

Assessment opportunity
After the whole-class work, children working at levels 2-3 can use the interactive activity 'Story outline', in which each paragraph has already been summarised. They can read the summaries and then put them in the correct sequence. Ensure they understand how to identify the start of a paragraph. Explain that the start of a line of dialogue does not necessarily represent the start of a new paragraph. Children working at levels 4-5 can use their own copies of the story extract from the photocopiable page to number the remaining paragraphs independently, find the key points and then to summarise each paragraph. They will then use the photocopiable page 'Story outline' to help them to summarise each paragraph. Assess whether children can identify the main points of each paragraph. Can children find key words or are they simply highlighting large chunks of text?

Assessment evidence
At levels 2-3, children will be able to sequence some information correctly. At levels 4-5, children will be able to identify relevant points from each paragraph and they will be able to describe these key points in the form of a summary. This activity will provide evidence towards Reading AF2.

Next steps
Support: Provide children with seven picture cards that depict the story *Beat the Bully* and seven corresponding summary statements on individual pieces of card. Play a Snap! game with the children where they practise matching summary statements, such as 'Billy is frightened of the beetle', with the correct pictures from the story.
Extension: Ask children to practise summarising key points as a homework exercise. Invite children to summarise the key points of what they read into a short paragraph to share with the class.

Key aspects of learning
Communication: Children will develop their ability to work collaboratively in pairs, groups or whole-class contexts. They will communicate outcomes orally, in writing and through use of ICT if appropriate.

Phase ② Holly's Worry

Learning outcome
Children can identify and discuss evidence that suggests the character's point of view.

Success criteria
I can find evidence in the text which suggests a character's point of view.

Setting the context
Introduce the whole class to the *The Worry Website* by Jacqueline Wilson which is a book of linked short stories. The children in Mr Speed's class have lots of worries so Mr Speed sets up a class Worry Website. Anyone in the class can enter their worry anonymously on the website and then wait for someone to type some advice. Each story tells of a different worry and how the problem got solved. Read the children the first story from the book *The Worry Website* (up to page 23). Invite them to explain the issues which Holly faces: (she doesn't want a new stepmum, she is sad that her own mother has left her, she wants her dad's girlfriend to be horrible so that she has an excuse to dislike her, she is jealous of her dad's affections for his new girlfriend, she is unhappy about the way her mother doesn't seem to care for her, she doesn't know how to stop behaving badly towards Miss Morgan).

Assessment opportunity
After shared reading of the book, invite the children to highlight examples in the text extract from the photocopiable page 'Holly's Worry' that give evidence of Holly's point of view. Ask them: *Which words in the text extract tell us what Holly thinks about fairy stories? What does Holly say that tells us how she feels about her dad? What does Holly say which shows us how she feels about Circle Time?* Demonstrate how to highlight only the relevant word/phrase and discuss what has been identified. Target particular children during the whole-class activity and observe whether they can locate relevant information in the text. If they are unable to identify the exact words in the text, can they describe the character's point of view in their own words?

Assessment evidence
At levels 2–3, children may select specific words from the text (for example, 'favourite', 'seriously cool') and they may paraphrase quotes from the text, for example, 'Holly says, fairy tales are cool'. At levels 4–5, children will identify mostly relevant points in the text and will support their comments with appropriate textual references. This activity will provide evidence towards Reading AF2.

Next steps
Support: Ask children further questions to help them to locate evidence, for example: *What does Holly say that tells you how she feels about her mum leaving home? What does Holly say that tells you how she feels about Mr Speed?*
Extension: Ask children to write an explanation of Holly's feelings using the evidence from the text. Explain how to present the highlighted text as quotes using speech marks.

Key aspects of learning
Reasoning: Children will discuss the influence of issues on characters, using evidence from the text to justify their opinions and referring to wider evidence from their own knowledge and experience.

NARRATIVE

Phase ② This is what I think...

Learning outcome
Children can discuss different characters' points of view.

Success criteria
● I can explain how different characters feel about an issue.
● I can give reasons for a character's feelings.

Setting the context
The children will need to have read the story 'Holly's Worry' from *The Worry Website*. Discuss Holly's point of view, and list on the board the different issues that she faces. List the other people who are involved in Holly's worry: (Hannah, her dad, her mum and Miss Morgan.) Using the 'jigsaw technique' for whole-class discussion, put the children into home groups of four and number them 1, 2, 3, 4. All the 1s will focus on Miss Morgan, all the 2s on Dad, all the 3s on Mum and all the 4s on Hannah. In their groups, the children should then discuss the different characters' points of view. Now rearrange them so all the same numbers are together. These 'expert' groups will then pool all the ideas about their allocated character. Children reform into their home groups and report back on the extra ideas they have gathered.

Assessment opportunity
Circulate around the groups during the jigsaw discussion. Ask questions to prompt the children to consider the viewpoints of the characters: *How do you think Dad feels about being on his own? Do you think it is difficult for him to bring up two girls without a partner? How do you think Miss Morgan feels when Holly is being horrible to her? Why doesn't Hannah feel the same way as Holly?* Make notes on the contributions children make during the group and whole-class discussions and relate this to their understanding of the text. Assess the children's oral responses in terms of how well they have made inferences from the textual evidence. Do their comments make actual reference to specific points in the text? Can children track how points of view change as events develop?

Assessment evidence
At levels 2–3, children will make simple inferences about how a character feels using evidence from the text. At levels 4–5, their comments may include inferences developed from evidence throughout the text. This activity will provide evidence towards Reading AF3.

Next steps
Support: Give the children the interactive activity 'Holly's Worry – points of view' before they carry out the discussion work to enable them to gain a greater understanding of other characters' points of view. Use the statements from the activity to use for support during the drama work.
Extension: Ask the children to write a letter to Holly in the role of one of the other characters explaining how they feel about the situation.

Key aspects of learning
Empathy: By taking part in role-play activities, children will be able to identify more closely with fictional characters and will be helped to understand their feelings and actions.
Social skills: When working collaboratively, children will listen to and respect other people's ideas. They will take on different roles in a group.
Communication: Children will develop their ability to work collaboratively in pairs, groups or whole-class contexts. They will communicate outcomes orally, in writing and through use of ICT if appropriate.
Reasoning: Children will discuss the influence of issues on characters, using evidence from the text to justify their opinions and referring to wider evidence from their own knowledge and experience.

Phase ② My advice is...

Learning outcome
Children can write giving advice to the main character.

Success criteria
- I can write a paragraph giving advice to a main character of a story.
- I can suggest sensible solutions for the character's problems.
- I can give reasons for my advice.

Setting the context
The children will need to have carried out the previous activity on page 59. Invite children to imagine that they are in Mr Speed's class and that they have read the anonymous worry (from Holly) on the Worry Website. Ask them to write a paragraph or a sentence giving Holly some advice. Explain that they are responding to Holly's typed-in worry: *I think I am getting a stepmother. I wish she was wicked.* Share the success criteria with the class to use during the peer-evaluation.

Assessment opportunity
Hand out the photocopiable page 'Advice for Holly'. Suggest the children start with: 'If I were you, I would...' and follow this with reasons for their advice. Then ask the children to swap work with a partner to read and to evaluate each other's advice. Assess whether children can empathise with the main character and make a relevant response, offering sensible solutions to her problems. Can they elaborate on why they are suggesting certain actions? Is their viewpoint consistent with the issues in the text? The children can then assess their peer's work in response to the success criteria. Ensure that they give positive responses (two ticks) and make a constructive comment on how to improve the piece of work (a wish).

Assessment evidence
At levels 2–3, children will include some relevant ideas in the writing but without the inclusion of a great amount of detail. At levels 4–5, children will have developed their ideas appropriately. They will have established a viewpoint and put this across fairly coherently. This activity will provide evidence towards Writing AF1.

Next steps
Support: Provide children with suggestions for advice for Holly. They can then explain why each piece of advice is useful by using qualifying connectives in their statements, for example, 'If I were Holly I would...because...' .
Extension: Encourage children to explain reasons for their given advice using more advanced connectives: '...in order to...' or '...so that...'.

Key aspects of learning
Social skills: When working collaboratively, children will listen to and respect other people's ideas. They will take on different roles in a group.

Phase ③ My Worry Website plan

Learning outcome
Children can use a setting, characters and an issue/dilemma to plan a story.

Success criteria
- I can explore a problem/issue and develop it to create a structure for my story.
- I can plan my story using a story planner.

Setting the context
The children will need to have explored stories that contain issues/dilemmas. Read more of the stories from *The Worry Website*, including the prize-winning story 'Lisa's Worry' written by Lauren Roberts, aged 12. Break down the structure of each story – identify what happened in the opening, the dilemma, the build-up, the conflict, the resolution and the ending.

Unit 4 ⬚ Stories which raise issues/dilemmas

Assessment opportunity

Explain that you would now like the children to imagine that they are in Mr Speed's class and they are sitting down to type their worry into the Worry Website. Provide the class with a list of characters and worries from the photocopiable page 'Mr Speed's class'. Alternatively they can make up their own worry and write it at the bottom of the sheet. Then give all the children the photocopiable page 'Story planner' and ask them to plan their Worry story. As the children are planning their stories, assess whether they are organising their ideas logically, indicating a clear story opening and ending, for example.

Assessment evidence

At levels 2-3, children's story plans will usually indicate ideas for an introduction and an ending to the story. At levels 4-5, children's story plans will be more organised and will include an appropriate introduction and ending. This activity will provide evidence towards Writing AF3.

Next steps

Support: For children who are struggling to consolidate their ideas into a plan provide them with the checklist from the photocopiable page 'Are you ready to write?'.

Extension: Stories about issues focus on the main character's feelings. These feelings change through the story. Encourage more confident learners to incorporate detail of their main character's feelings into their story plan by using the photocopiable page 'My character's feelings and actions'.

Key aspects of learning

Communication: They will communicate outcomes orally, in writing and through use of ICT if appropriate.

Phase ③ My Worry Website story

Learning outcome
Children can write a longer story in paragraphs.

Success criteria
- I can write a story about a dilemma using paragraphs for each stage of the story.
- I can show how the main character feels by describing his or her actions.
- I can use dialogue in my story to develop the plot.

Setting the context

This activity assumes the children have carried out the previous activity above. Ensure the children have completed the planning stage and are comfortable with the content and structure of their Worry Website stories. Reinforce the fact that they are writing in role as a character in Mr Speed's class and so will be writing in the first person, using 'my', 'me', 'I' and so on. Display the main success criteria: to write a story...using paragraphs for each stage - do not overload the class with too many other aspects. Provide plenty of time for extended writing.

Assessment opportunity

Ask the children to develop their story from their original plan and assess how well they achieve this. Is each stage of the story presented in separate paragraphs? How are the paragraphs being linked?

Assessment evidence

At levels 2-3, children will mostly link the sections of their stories by the use of pronouns. At levels 4-5, children will use paragraphs to organise the material in their stories and each paragraph will usually be linked, for example, by the use of time connectives. This activity will provide evidence towards Writing AF4.

Next steps

Support: Suggest children write each paragraph in a separate box, in a supported

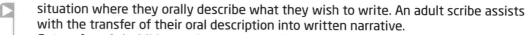
situation where they orally describe what they wish to write. An adult scribe assists with the transfer of their oral description into written narrative.

Extension: Ask children to look at where they could increase the atmosphere in their stories by describing the weather or the passing of time to evoke and support the feelings and actions of the characters. For example, describing grey clouds blotting out the sun, to help create a dismal mood.

Key aspects of learning

Communication: They will communicate outcomes orally, in writing and through use of ICT if appropriate.

Phase ③ Editorial reviews

Learning outcome
Children can carry out peer assessment of each other's stories.

Success criteria
- I can review stories written by my peers.
- I can identify the issue in my peer's story.
- I can make constructive comments to help them to improve their work.

Setting the context
Select a number of stories written by children in the class (photocopied anonymously or agreed with the authors) to use for peer assessment. Display one of the stories and read it to the class. Model how to review the story using the checklist of more detailed success criteria on the photocopiable page 'Editorial review' and explain to the children that it is helpful to 'think aloud' while critiquing.

Assessment opportunity
Divide the children up into mixed ability 'review panels' to carry out peer assessment of the stories in the light of the specific success criteria. Circulate round the groups and listen to their comments. Are they being constructive? Are they picking out features which directly relate to the success criteria? Can they make constructive comments to help the author improve their writing? This activity will help to develop the children as independent learners who can give each other valuable feedback so they learn from and support each other. The activity will also provide the children with an opportunity to hold discussions in groups.

Assessment evidence
At levels 2-3, children will make statements about their likes and dislikes of their peers' stories and will sometimes provide reasons for their comments. At levels 4-5, children will identify and comment on the main purpose of their peers' stories. This activity will provide evidence towards Reading AF6.

Next steps
Support: Give children a copy of a suitable story and provide them with features to find and highlight. For example: *Can you find where the writer has started a paragraph? Can you find a sentence which tells you how the main character is feeling?*
Extension: Where children have identified areas for improvement, invite them to rewrite individual sentences or paragraphs. Then ask them to explain why their contribution is an improvement in terms of the success criteria specified. For example: *How could the author have shown that the main character was frightened by describing her actions?*

Key aspects of learning
Social skills: When working collaboratively, children will listen to and respect other people's ideas. They will take on different roles in a group.
Communication: Children will develop their ability to work collaboratively in pairs, groups or whole-class contexts. They will communicate outcomes orally, in writing and through ICT if appropriate.

NARRATIVE

Periodic assessment

Reading

Learning outcome
Children can identify how an opening paragraph can introduce a main character and trigger an issue.

Success criteria
- I can identify the issue in a story.
- I can identify whether the story is written in the first or third person.
- I can identify the trigger point the author uses to introduce the issue.
- I can identify the style that is used to create the trigger.

Setting the context
Children will need to have knowledge of the main features of dilemma stories and appropriate writing styles. Present the children with the opening paragraphs from four stories with dilemmas/issues. Tell them that they are going to identify and compare the features of these opening paragraphs.

Assessment opportunity
Hand out the photocopiable page 'Narrative 4 Reading assessment text' and 'Narrative 4 Reading assessment'. Ask the children to read the opening paragraphs of the four stories and to then complete the analysis grid.

Assessment evidence
The children will make relevant points about what is contained in the texts; make inferences from the evidence in the text and identify the purpose of the language used and the effect on the reader. This activity will facilitate gathering evidence against Reading AF2, AF3 and AF6. Use this activity and other examples from this unit to assess their overall progress in Reading.

Writing

Learning outcome
Children can write an opening to a story with an issue using a trigger point.

Success criteria
- I can write an introductory paragraph that ends with a link to the next stage of the story.
- I can write in the third or first person.
- I can use a trigger point to initiate a dilemma/issue.
- I can decide on the style for my trigger point (eg direct speech, a question).

Setting the context
The children will need to have carried out the activity above. Ask them to write a story introduction on the photocopiable page 'Narrative 4 Writing assessment' using a 'trigger' to initiate a dilemma/issue. They should decide how to introduce the trigger, for example, through use of a question (How was I to know that Mr Brown was on the other side of the fence?).

Assessment opportunity
Ask questions to establish if children have thought through the development of their characters, the dilemma/issue and how it is to be introduced. Are they writing consistently in the first or the third person?

Assessment evidence
At levels 2-3, children's stories will mostly include relevant ideas. At levels 4-5, their story content will be more appropriate and developed. This activity will provide evidence against Writing AF1. Use this activity and examples of children's work during this unit to assess their overall progress in Writing.

NARRATIVE

Name _____ Date _____

Story outline

- Read the story extract, identify where each paragraph starts and number them.
- Summarise the key points of each paragraph below to give an outline of the story.

Paragraph number	Stage of story	Key points summary
1		
2		
3		
4		
5		
6		
7		

Story stages:

Opening	Build-up	Conflict	Ending linked to opening
Dilemma/issue	Key action	Resolution	

Red ⬤ Amber ⬤ Green ⬤

I can summarise the key points in each paragraph to produce a story outline. ☐

NARRATIVE

Advice for Holly

The Worry Website

Type in your worry:

I think I'm going to get a stepmother.

I wish she was wicked.

Advice:

_____

_____

_____

_____

_____

✔ _____

✔ _____

 _____

Mr Speed's class

- Choose a pupil from Mr Speed's class (or write your own worry below).
- Plan a story about their worry using the story planner.

Name: Jodie

Worry: I'm new to the school and it's the middle of term. I don't know my way around or where anything is. Everyone is in groups of friends and I feel very lonely and confused.

Name: Ben

Worry: I live with my mum and my little brother, Sam. Dad left home and mum has to work in the supermarket in the evenings and at weekends. I am left at home looking after Sam and have to do all the chores. I wish I could be out playing with my friends. I want to help Mum and my family but I want to be a kid too!

Name: Toni

Worry: Last night my friend and I were playing football and we broke a pane in old Mr Digby's greenhouse. We should have owned up then but now it's too late. We are so scared of being in real trouble.

Name: Sally

Worry: I copied my friend's maths because I was too embarrassed to admit that I was struggling and now I can't do any of the work in class. It's getting worse and worse!

Name: _____

Worry: _____

_____

Illustration © Bill Houston/Bill Houston Creative Limited.

NARRATIVE
UNIT 5 Plays

Literacy objectives

Speak and listen for a wide range of purposes in different contexts
Strand 1 Speaking
- Use and reflect on some ground rules for sustaining talk and interactions.

Strand 4 Drama
- Create roles showing how behaviour can be interpreted from different viewpoints.
- Develop scripts based on improvisation.
- Comment constructively on plays and performances, discussing effects and how they are achieved.

Read and write for a range of purposes on paper and on screen
Strand 7 Understanding and interpreting texts
- Deduce characters' reasons for behaviour from their actions and explain how ideas are developed in non-fiction texts.
- Explain how writers use figurative and expressive language to create images and atmosphere.

Strand 9 Creating and shaping texts
- Develop and refine ideas in writing using planning and problem-solving strategies.
- Show imagination through the language used to create emphasis, humour, atmosphere or suspense.
- Choose and combine words, images and other features for particular effects.

Strand 11 Sentence structure and punctuation
- Clarify meaning and point of view by using varied sentence structure (phrases, clauses and adverbials).

Strand 12 Presentation
- Write consistently with neat, legible and joined handwriting.

Key aspects of learning

Enquiry
- Children will need to draw conclusions and evaluate outcomes.

Creative thinking
- Children will generate imaginative ideas in response to stimuli. They will discover and make connections through play and experimentation. They will be encouraged to look at and think about things differently and from other points of view. They should apply imaginative thinking to achieve an objective and reflect critically on ideas, actions and outcomes.

Information processing
- Children will record information using a given format and using formats they have devised.

Reasoning
- Children will predict and anticipate events. They should use the language of sequence.

Evaluation
- Children will be encouraged to express their own views, opinions and preferences and evaluate the quality of an outcome.

Assessment focuses

Reading
AF2 (*understand, describe, select or retrieve information, events or ideas from texts and use quotation and reference to text*).
AF3 (*deduce, infer or interpret information, events or ideas from texts*).
AF4 (*identify and comment on the structure and organisation of texts, including grammatical and presentational features at text level*).
AF5 (*explain and comment on writers' use of language, including grammatical and literary features at word and sentence level*).

Writing
AF2 (*produce texts which are appropriate to task, reader and purpose*).

Speaking and listening
Speaking (speak with clarity, intonation and pace).
Drama (improvise and sustain roles; plan, perform and evaluate plays; work with others in performance).

Resources

Phase 1 activities
Photocopiable page, 'Granny, I'm home!'
Photocopiable page, 'Playscript checklist'
Interactive activity, 'Features of a playscript'
Interactive activity, 'Selecting adverbs – stage directions'
Photocopiable page, 'Mime cards'
Phase 2 activities
Photocopiable page, 'Holly's Worry – role play'
Photocopiable pages, 'Playscript' (versions 1 and 2)
Phase 3 activities
Photocopiable page, 'Holly's Worry – dialogue and adverbs'
Photocopiable page, 'Holly's Worry – my playscript'
Photocopiable page, 'Performance evaluation'
Periodic assessment
Photocopiable page, 'Narrative 5 Reading assessment text'
Photocopiable page, 'Narrative 5 Reading assessment'
Photocopiable page, 'Narrative 5 Writing assessment'

Unit 5 ⬛ Plays

Learning outcomes	Assessment opportunity and evidence	Assessment focuses (AFs)		Success criteria
		Level 2	Level 3	
Phase ① activities pages 73-74				
Features of a playscript Children understand the conventions of playscripts.	• Independent activity where children use the interactive activity to identify and sort playscript features. • Completed interactive activity.	**Reading AF4** Some awareness of use of features of organisation.	**Reading AF4** A few basic features of organisation at text level identified, with little or no linked comment.	I can recognise the features of a playscript.
Following stage directions Children understand the role of stage directions.	• Whole-class activity where children mime stage directions to illustrate adverbs. • Independent activity where children use the interactive activity to select adverbs. • Children's performances and the completed interactive activity.	**Reading AF5** Some effective language choices noted.	**Reading AF5** A few basic features of writer's use of language identified, but with little or no comment.	I can recognise and use adverbs in stage directions.
Phase ② activities pages 74-76				
Holly's Worry – scene one Children can use known characters and issues to improvise a scene.	• Paired activity where children improvise a scene from *The Worry Website*. • Children's improvisations and teacher's observation.	**Reading AF3** Simple, plausible inference about events and information, using evidence from text.	**Reading AF3** • Straightforward inference based on a single point of reference in the text. • Responses to text show meaning established at a literal level.	I can work with a partner to improvise a dialogue between two known characters.
Holly's Worry – a playscript Children can write a simple playscript with stage directions using their improvised scene.	• Supported activity where children write a playscript scene. • Completed playscripts.	**Writing AF2** • Some basic purpose established. • Some appropriate features of the given form used. • Some attempts to adopt appropriate style.	**Writing AF2** • Purpose established at a general level. • Main features of selected form sometimes signalled to the reader. • Some attempts at appropriate style, with attention to reader.	• I can use my improvisation to write a short playscript. • I can use adverbs in my stage directions.
Holly and Hannah – take one! Children can perform using their playscripts.	• Paired activity where children swap, perform and discuss each other's playscripts. • Children's performances and oral responses.	**Reading AF3** Simple, plausible inference about events and information, using evidence from text.	**Reading AF3** • Straightforward inference based on a single point of reference in the text. • Responses to text show meaning established at a literal level.	I can use my peer's playscript to perform a short scene.
Phase ③ activities pages 76-78				
Narrative to playscript Children can develop a playscript from a piece of narrative.	• Independent activity where children highlight direct speech and select suitable adverbs. • Annotated photocopiable pages.	**Reading AF2** • Some specific, straightforward information recalled. • Generally clear idea of where to look for information.	**Reading AF2** • Simple, most obvious points identified though there may also be some misunderstanding. • Some comments include quotations from or references to text, but not always relevant.	• I can identify the dialogue and the speaker in a story. • I can choose the adverbs required to help me to write stage directions.

Unit 5 📖 Plays

Learning outcomes	Assessment opportunity and evidence	Assessment focuses (AFs)		Success criteria
		Level 2	Level 3	
The final playscript Children can develop a playscript from a piece of narrative.	● Independent activity where children write their own playscripts. ● Children's completed playscripts and teacher's observations.	**Writing AF2** ● Some basic purpose established. ● Some appropriate features of the given form used. ● Some attempts to adopt appropriate style.	**Writing AF2** ● Purpose established at a general level. ● Main features of selected form sometimes signalled to the reader. ● Some attempts at appropriate style, with attention to reader.	● I can use dialogue from a story in my playscript. ● I can include adverbs in my stage directions.
Performance evaluation Children can perform, record and evaluate their plays using ICT.	● Group activity where children evaluate performances of playscripts. ● Peer assessment and completed evaluation forms.	**Reading AF3** ● Simple, plausible inference about events and information, using evidence from text. ● Comments based on textual cues, sometimes misunderstood.	**Reading AF3** ● Straightforward inference based on a single point of reference in the text. ● Responses to text show meaning established at a literal level.	● I can perform using a playscript. ● I can evaluate my own and others' performances.

Learning outcomes	Assessment opportunity and evidence	Assessment focuses (AFs)		Success criteria
		Level 4	Level 5	
Phase ① activities pages 73-74				
Features of a playscript Children understand the conventions of playscripts.	● Independent activity where children read a text extract to identify and sort playscript features. ● Annotated photocopiable pages.	**Reading AF4** ● Some structural choices identified with simple comment. ● Some basic features of organisation at text level identified.	**Reading AF4** ● Comments show some awareness of writer's craft. ● Various features relating to organisation at text level, including form, are clearly identified.	I can recognise the features of a playscript.
Following stage directions Children understand the role of stage directions.	● Whole-class activity where children mime stage directions to illustrate adverbs. ● Children's performances.	**Reading AF5** ● Some basic features of writer's use of language identified. ● Simple comments on writer's choices.	**Reading AF5** ● Various features of writer's use of language identified, with some explanation. ● Comments show some awareness of the effect of writer's language choices.	I can recognise and use adverbs in stage directions.
Phase ② activities pages 74-76				
Holly's Worry – scene one Children can use known characters and issues to improvise a scene.	● Paired activity where children improvise a scene from *The Worry Website*. ● Children's improvisations and teacher's observation.	**Reading AF3** ● Comments make inferences based on evidence from different points in the text. ● Inferences often correct, but comments are not always rooted securely in the text or repeat narrative or content.	**Reading AF3** ● Comments develop explanation of inferred meanings drawing on evidence across the text. ● Comments make inferences and deductions based on textual evidence.	I can work with a partner to improvise a dialogue between two known characters.
Holly's Worry – a playscript Children can write a simple playscript with stage directions using their improvised scene.	● Independent activity where children write a playscript scene. ● Children's completed playscripts.	**Writing AF2** ● Main purpose of writing is clear but not always consistently maintained. ● Main features of selected form are clear and appropriate to purpose. ● Style generally appropriate to task, though awareness of reader not always sustained.	**Writing AF2** ● Main purpose of writing is clear and consistently maintained. ● Features of selected form clearly established with some adaptation to purpose. ● Appropriate style clearly established to maintain reader's interest throughout.	● I can use my improvisation to write a short playscript. ● I can use adverbs in my stage directions.

Unit 5 📖 Plays

Learning outcomes	Assessment opportunity and evidence	Assessment focuses (AFs)		Success criteria
		Level 4	Level 5	
Holly and Hannah – take one! Children can perform using their playscripts.	• Paired activity where children swap, perform and discuss each other's playscripts. • Children's performances and oral responses.	**Reading AF3** • Comments make inferences based on evidence from different points in the text. • Inferences often correct, but comments are not always rooted securely in the text or repeat narrative or content.	**Reading AF3** • Comments develop explanation of inferred meanings drawing on evidence across the text. • Comments make inferences and deductions based on textual evidence.	I can use my peer's playscript to perform a short scene.

Phase ③ activities pages 76–78

Learning outcomes	Assessment opportunity and evidence	Level 4	Level 5	Success criteria
Narrative to playscript Children can develop a playscript from a piece of narrative.	• Independent activity where children highlight direct speech and select suitable adverbs. • Annotated photocopiable pages.	**Reading AF2** • Some relevant points identified. • Comments supported by some generally relevant textual reference or quotation.	**Reading AF2** • Most relevant points clearly identified, including those selected from different places in the text. • Comments generally supported by relevant textual reference of quotation, even when points made are not always accurate.	• I can identify the dialogue and the speaker in a story. • I can choose the adverbs required to help me to write stage directions.
The final playscript Children can develop a playscript from a piece of narrative.	• Independent activity where children write their own playscripts. • Children's completed playscripts and teacher's observations.	**Writing AF2** • Main purpose of writing is clear but not always consistently maintained . • Main features of selected form are clear and appropriate to purpose. • Style generally appropriate to task, though awareness of reader not always sustained.	**Writing AF2** • Main purpose of writing is clear and consistently maintained. • Features of selected form clearly established with some adaptation to purpose . • Appropriate style clearly established to maintain reader's interest throughout.	• I can use dialogue from a story in my playscript. • I can include adverbs in my stage directions.
Performance evaluation Children can perform, record and evaluate their plays using ICT.	• Group activity where children evaluate performances of playscripts. • Peer assessment and completed evaluation forms.	**Reading AF3** • Comments make inferences based on evidence from different points in the text. • Inferences often correct, but comments are not always rooted securely in the text or repeat narrative or content.	**Reading AF3** • Comments develop explanation of inferred meanings drawing on evidence across the text. • Comments make inferences and deductions based on textual evidence.	• I can perform using a playscript. • I can evaluate my own and others' performances.

Phase ① Features of a playscript

Learning outcome
Children understand the conventions of playscripts.

Success criteria
I can recognise the features of a playscript.

Setting the context
Ensure that the children are comfortable with the conventions of playscripts - direct speech, stage directions, scenes and so on. Children will annotate an excerpt from a playscript and will identify the different features of playscripts.

Assessment opportunity
Children working at levels 2-3 will use the interactive activity 'Features of a playscript'. Children can read the text and drag and drop the different playscript features to annotate the text. Children working at levels 4-5 will use the playscript extract from the photocopiable pages 'Granny, I'm home!' and 'Playscript checklist'. Ask them to read the extract and use different colours to highlight all the different features listed in the checklist. Encourage the children to comment further on some of the features by asking: *Why is it important to know that Granny is Australian?* Assess the children's knowledge of the organisational features of a playscript.

Assessment evidence
At levels 2-3, children will be able to identify a few features of organisation in the playscript. At levels 4-5, children will be able to comment on the features of the playscript. The activity will provide evidence against Reading AF4.

Next steps
Support: Focus on plays during guided reading sessions. By reading further plays, children will gain the opportunity to reinforce their understanding of the features of playscripts.
Extension: Read plays aloud during guided reading and encourage children to explain how they would translate the play into a performance.

Key aspects of learning
Enquiry: Children will need to draw conclusions and evaluate outcomes.

Phase ① Following stage directions

Learning outcome
Children understand the role of stage directions.

Success criteria
I can recognise and use adverbs in stage directions.

Setting the context
The children should be aware of the definition of an adverb and should have practised using them in sentence-level work. The children will work as a whole class, with support being given to children working at levels 2-3. Prepare the word cards from the photocopiable page 'Mime cards'. Cut out and place the mime cards in one container and the adverb cards in another.

Assessment opportunity
Ask the children to take one of each word card and then act out the mime in the style suggested by the adverb. The rest of the class can interpret what the action was and how it was being carried out. Write the corresponding stage direction on the board, for example: 'Actor brushes hair angrily'. Repeat the activity with different children who you are targeting for assessment. Question the children about the adverb they picked, for example: *Is 'craftily' a good word to use to describe the way the actor washes up? What adverb would you use to show that*

NARRATIVE

▶ *the actor didn't want to wash up?* Assess how well the children interpret the written instruction. Following the drama work, use the interactive activity 'Selecting adverbs - stage directions' and ask the children to give reasons for their choices. Assess how well the children note appropriate language choices.

Assessment evidence
At levels 2-3, children will demonstrate through their mimes that they understand how some adverbs affect verbs. They will select some of the correct adverbs on the interactive activity. At levels 4-5, children will be able to suggest and use effective adverbs and they will be able to select the correct adverbs for the interactive activity. They will also be able to give reasons for their choices. The children's mimes, verbal responses and completed interactive activities will provide evidence against Reading AF5.

Next steps
Support: Carry out dictionary work to establish the meanings of common adverbs. Discuss examples of when they may be used.
Extension: Carry out thesaurus work to find synonyms for adverbs and to broaden children's vocabulary range.

Key aspects of learning
Enquiry: Children will need to draw conclusions and evaluate outcomes.
Creative thinking: Children will generate imaginative ideas in response to stimuli. They will discover and make connections through play and experimentation. They will be encouraged to look at and think about things differently and from other points of view. They should apply imaginative thinking to achieve an objective and reflect critically on ideas, actions and outcomes.

Phase ② Holly's Worry - scene one

Learning outcome
Children can use known characters and issues to improvise a scene.

Success criteria
I can work with a partner to improvise a dialogue between two known characters.

Setting the context
The extract used in this activity links to Narrative Unit 4 Stories which raise issues/dilemmas (see page 59). If Unit 4 has already been carried out, children will be familiar with Holly's worries and will know the characters. However, if they have not studied Unit 4 prior to this work, use the introduction and text extract on the photocopiable page 'Holly's Worry - role play' to introduce the scenario and the characters. Children will work in pairs matched by ability.

Assessment opportunity
Give the pairs of children a copy of the photocopiable page 'Holly's Worry- role play'. Tell them to read the extract and then to improvise a scene between the two sisters, Holly and Hannah. They should discuss the pros and cons of having Miss Morgan as their new stepmother. Ask the children: *How is Holly feeling about the idea of having a new mother? How do you know? Why is she trying to convince her sister to feel the same way that she does? Why do you think Hannah is happy to have Miss Morgan as their new mother?* This activity will provide the opportunity to assess a child's ability to use inference. Observe the children's improvisations to see how well they have interpreted the text and inferred the different characters' points of view.

Assessment evidence
At levels 2-3, children will make simple or straightforward inferences using evidence from the text, such as 'I think Holly is scared because she says "I am scared she's going to live with us". 'At levels 4-5, children will make inferences from different points in the text, such as 'Holly doesn't want Miss Morgan to take her mum's place.'

She says "it's not fair" and then later she says "No, we've got a mother already." This activity gathers evidence towards Reading AF3.

Next steps
Support: Re-read the text taking each piece of dialogue individually and ask what children think that these words tell you about how the character is feeling.
Extension: Ask children to think about some possible stage directions to help portray the different characters' feelings.

Key aspects of learning
Creative thinking: Children will generate imaginative ideas in response to stimuli. They will discover and make connections through play and experimentation. They will be encouraged to look at and think about things differently and from other points of view. They should apply imaginative thinking to achieve an objective and reflect critically on ideas, actions and outcomes.

Phase ② Holly's Worry – a playscript

Learning outcome
Children can write a simple playscript with stage directions using their improvised scene.

Success criteria
- I can use my improvisation to write a short playscript.
- I can use adverbs in my stage directions.

Setting the context
Using the improvised scene from the previous activity, children will work individually to write a short scene using the conventions of a playscript. Hand out versions 1 and 2 of the playscript template.

Assessment opportunity
Children working at levels 2-3 will use version 1 of the template from the photocopiable page 'Playscript' to write their playscript and those working at levels 4-5 will use version 2 of the photocopiable page. Encourage them to consider how they acted during their improvisation. How could they write this as a stage direction? Have they described the props they would use? Have they shown who is speaking and used colons to signal speech? Gather up the completed playscripts at the end of the activity.

Assessment evidence
At levels 2-3, children will be able to write a playscript using some appropriate features of the genre. At levels 4-5, children will be able to use the main features of playscripts and their style of writing will be mostly appropriate. The completed playscripts provide evidence against Writing AF2.

Next steps
Support: Ask children to recap their improvisation, stopping them at appropriate points and recording this as dialogue.
Extension: Children could extend their play to include a second scene where Dad enters to find out why the girls aren't asleep.

Key aspects of learning
Creative thinking: Children will generate imaginative ideas in response to stimuli. They will discover and make connections through play and experimentation. They will be encouraged to look at and think about things differently and from other points of view. They should apply imaginative thinking to achieve an objective and reflect critically on ideas, actions and outcomes.
Information processing: Children will record information using a given format and using formats they have devised.

NARRATIVE

Phase ② Holly and Hannah – take one!

Learning outcome
Children can perform using their playscripts.

Success criteria
I can use my peer's playscript to perform a short scene.

Setting the context
The children will need to have completed their playscripts from the previous activity. They will work in same-ability pairs and act out playscripts written by their peers. Choose and copy a select number of the children's playscripts and hand them out to the different pairs (making sure that no one has their own playscript) – in this way comparisons can be made regarding the children's interpretations of the scripts.

Assessment opportunity
Ask the pairs to read their playscripts carefully to themselves, and then ask each pair to read their playscript out in turn, with suitable dramatic interpretation. Afterwards, ask the children questions regarding their performance: *How was Holly feeling? How do you know this from the playscript?* Listen for comments that show whether they can make inferences regarding the intentions of the playscripts. Observe whether any of the children's actions were carried out in response to the directions in the script. Do the performances demonstrate that children have interpreted the directions and words in the playscript?

Assessment evidence
At levels 2–3, children will make simple or straightforward inferences on how the characters were feeling. At levels 4–5, children will make inferences on how characters were feeling throughout the performance and provide reasons for these inferences – 'Holly was feeling jealous because she said "she wants to be her dad's special girlfriend" and then later in the play she was speaking in a sulky voice'. This activity will provide evidence against Reading AF3.

Next steps
Support: Carry out further drama games to help children to develop their ability to empathise with the situations different characters are in.
Extension: Children could act out any extra scenes that had been written from the previous activity in the same way.

Key aspects of learning
Creative thinking: Children will generate imaginative ideas in response to stimuli. They will discover and make connections through play and experimentation. They will be encouraged to look at and think about things differently and from other points of view. They should apply imaginative thinking to achieve an objective and reflect critically on ideas, actions and outcomes.

Phase ③ Narrative to playscript

Learning outcome
Children can develop a playscript from a piece of narrative.

Success criteria
● I can identify the dialogue and the speaker in a story.
● I can choose the adverbs required to help me to write stage directions.

Setting the context
Recap the conventions of speech in narrative, and ensure that children are comfortable with the definition and uses of adverbs. Tell them that they are going to use this knowledge eventually to help them convert a story extract into a playscript. Children will need the text extract on the photocopiable page 'Holly's Worry – role play' from the previous activity above.

Assessment opportunity

Hand out the extract from the photocopiable page 'Holly's Worry – dialogue and adverbs'. Ask the children to highlight the words that are spoken by different characters, using a different colour for each character. They should then decide on adverbs to describe how the words should be spoken to assist them when writing stage directions. They can note these in the margins. As children are working, circulate and check whether they can identify relevant aspects of the text: Have children highlighted the actual words that are spoken? Do they know how to identify the direct speech? Have they chosen adverbs appropriately?

Assessment evidence

At levels 2–3, children will have identified some of the direct speech correctly and will have specified some simple adverbs. At levels 4–5, children will have identified most of the direct speech and will have included appropriate adverbs.
This activity enables assessment against Reading AF2.

Next steps

Support: Recap the rules for writing speech in narrative by writing a sentence of dialogue. Children can then highlight the actual words that are spoken.
Extension: Encourage children to look up their adverbs in a thesaurus to widen their vocabulary choices. Can they find new word choices that are more appropriate?

Key aspects of learning

Information processing: Children will record information using a given format and using formats they have devised.

Phase ③ The final playscript

Learning outcome
Children can develop a playscript from a piece of narrative.

Success criteria
● I can use dialogue from a story in my playscript.
● I can include adverbs in my stage directions.

Setting the context
Children will need to have completed the previous activity above. Tell them that they will use their highlighted story extracts and the ideas for adverbs to write a playscript. Check that they are happy with all the conventions of writing a script and recap if necessary.

Assessment opportunity
Hand out the playscript template on the photocopiable page 'Holly's Worry – my playscript' and ensure children have their annotated text extracts to hand. Ask them to use their annotations and the template to write their own playscript. Remind them to insert stage directions where they consider the actors may need them to assist with how they should speak and what they should do. Tell them they should also describe the props and costumes the characters will need. If stage directions are sparse, prompt children by asking what the character is doing and how they are speaking at different points in the script. Observe the children's ability to write with a clear purpose and appropriate style; whether they have included and established all the features of the genre in their writing and whether the reader (ie the actor) has been considered. Gather the finished playscripts when they are complete.

Assessment evidence
At levels 2–3, children will include some features of playscripts and will make an attempt to use the appropriate style. At levels 4–5, children will use the main features of playscripts and their writing style will be mostly appropriate. This activity provides the opportunity to gather evidence against Writing AF2.

▷ **Next steps**
Support: Provide children with the speech, props, costumes, character list and stage directions cut up in strips. Children use these to construct their playscript.
Extension: Children could incorporate a narrator's role into their play.

Key aspects of learning
Information processing: Children will record information using a given format and using formats they have devised.

Phase ③ Performance evaluation

Learning outcome
Children can perform, record and evaluate their plays using ICT.

Success criteria
● I can perform using a playscript.
● I can evaluate my own and others' performances.

Setting the context
Children will need to have written their playscripts from the previous activity. They will need to select a playscript to perform. Tell the children that they are going to film a performance of their playscript. They will have to work in small mixed ability groups to make the film, and then they will watch each other's films and make constructive suggestions for changes or improvements.

Assessment opportunity
Arrange children in groups of four, and ask them to decide on two actors, a camera person and a film director. Tell the children to rehearse the scene using one of the group's playscripts and then to film it using Digital Blue™ video cameras or whatever filming equipment is available. Each group can then evaluate a different group's performance against their written script and can use the photocopiable page 'Performance evaluation' to record their feedback. Remind children to be constructive in their comments and to provide sensible suggestions for improvements. Circulate among the groups, asking prompt questions such as: *Did the performance follow the stage directions on the playscript? How well do you think the actors took on the roles described?* Listen to the children's comments and assess whether they are able to infer how well a script has been interpreted as a performance.

Assessment evidence
This activity encourages children to develop their ability to carry out peer assessment. Use the children's written evaluations against the playscript and their verbal responses to provide evidence against Reading AF3.

Next steps
Support: Help children to carry out their assessments by asking leading questions.
Extension: Encourage children to write a review of a book that they have read that has been made into a film. They should consider how well the narrative has been interpreted by the directors and actors.

Key aspects of learning
Evaluation: Children will be encouraged to express their own views, opinions and preferences and evaluate the quality of an outcome.

NARRATIVE

Mime cards

Mimes

actor eats spaghetti	**actor brushes hair**	**actor eats an ice cream**
actor sweeps the floor	**actor writes a letter**	**actor walks a tightrope**
actor does the washing-up	**actor rocks a baby**	**actor cleans the windows**

Adverbs

confidently	**dreamily**	**anxiously**
angrily	**cheerfully**	**thoughtfully**
sleepily	**wildly**	**craftily**

NON-FICTION

UNIT 1 Recounts: newspapers/magazines

Literacy objectives

Speak and listen for a wide range of purposes in different contexts
Strand 1 Speaking
● Tell stories effectively and convey detailed information coherently for listeners.
Strand 2 Listening and responding
● Compare the different contributions of music, words and images in short extracts from TV programmes.

Read and write for a range of purposes on paper and on screen
Strand 7 Understanding and interpreting texts
● Deduce characters' reasons for behaviour from their actions and explain how ideas are developed in non-fiction texts.
Strand 8 Engaging with and responding to texts
● Interrogate texts to deepen and clarify understanding and response.
Strand 9 Creating and shaping texts
● Develop and refine ideas in writing using planning and problem-solving strategies.
● Use settings and characterisation to engage readers' interest.
Strand 10 Text structure and organisation
● Organise text into paragraphs to distinguish between different information, events or processes.
Strand 12 Presentation
● Use word-processing packages to present written work and continue to increase speed and accuracy in typing.

Key aspects of learning

Enquiry
● Children will be learning to ask who? what? where? when? and why? when researching a news story for a written or oral report.
Information processing
● Children will be identifying relevant information from a range of multi-media sources and using this as a basis for both planning and writing.
Reasoning
● Children will develop judgements on what is 'fact' and what is 'opinion' based on available evidence.
Communication
● Children will develop their ability to discuss the content and presentation of the news reports they are reading and writing. They will often work collaboratively in pairs and groups. They will communicate outcomes orally, in writing and through ICT.

Assessment focuses

Reading

AF2 (*understand, describe, select or retrieve information, events or ideas from texts and use quotation and reference to text*).

AF3 (*deduce, infer or interpret information, events or ideas from texts*).

AF4 (*identify and comment on the structure and organisation of texts, including grammatical and presentational features at text level*).

AF5 (*explain and comment on writers' use of language, including grammatical and literary features at word and sentence level*).

Writing

AF2 (*produce texts which are appropriate to task, reader and purpose*).

AF3 (*organise and present whole texts effectively, sequencing and structuring information, ideas and events*).

Speaking and listening

Speaking (recount information in an organised manner with relevant detail).

Listening and responding (respond to questions appropriately).

Resources

Phase 1 activities
Photocopiable page, 'My trip to London'
Interactive activity, 'My trip to London'
Photocopiable page, 'Recount timeline'
Phase 2 activities
Photocopiable pages, 'Fact or opinion?' (versions 1 and 2)
Interactive activity, 'Fact or opinion?'
Phase 3 activities
Photocopiable page, 'Features of a newspaper article'
Photocopiable page, 'Pronouns'
Phase 4 activities
Interactive activity, 'Trapped terrier's amazing rescue'
Photocopiable page, 'Graphic organiser'
Photocopiable pages, 'Newspaper article'
Photocopiable page, 'Newspaper article review'
Periodic assessment
Photocopiable page, 'Non-fiction 1 Reading assessment text'
Photocopiable page, 'Non-fiction 1 Reading assessment'

Unit 1 🔲 Recounts: newspapers/magazines

Learning outcomes	Assessment opportunity and evidence	Assessment focuses (AFs)		Success criteria
		Level 2	Level 3	
Phase ① activities pages 87-88				
My trip to London Children can organise and sequence a recount, identifying key events.	• Supported activity where children use a recount text to sequence photographs and captions in the interactive activity. • Completed interactive activity.	**Reading AF2** • Some specific, straightforward information recalled. • Generally clear idea of where to look for information.	**Reading AF2** • Simple, most obvious points identified though there may also be some misunderstanding. • Some comments include quotations from or references to text, but not always relevant.	I can sequence the key events of a recount.
Our school trip Children can write a draft recount in the correct verb tense.	• Independent activity where children draft a recount using a timeline. • Children's draft recount timeline.	**Writing AF3** • Some basic sequencing of ideas or material. • Openings and/or closings sometimes signalled.	**Writing AF3** • Some attempt to organise ideas with related points placed next to each other. • Some attempt to sequence ideas or material logically.	• I can plan my recount using a timeline, connectives and question words. • I can write a draft recount in the first person. • I can use the past tense in my writing.
Phase ② activities pages 89-90				
Fact or opinion? Children can orally distinguish between factual information and opinions based on factual information.	• Independent activity where children use the recount text or the interactive activity to identify facts and opinions. • Completed photocopiable pages or interactive activity.	**Reading AF3** • Simple, plausible inference about events and information, using evidence from text. • Comments based on textual cues, sometimes misunderstood.	**Reading AF3** • Straightforward inference based on a single point of reference in the text. • Responses to text show meaning established at a literal level or based on personal speculation.	• I can find examples of facts in a text. • I can find examples of opinions in a text.
Finding facts and opinions Children can identify and record factual information and opinions based on factual information.	• Paired activity where children identify facts and opinions in a newspaper article. • Completed photocopiable pages.	**Reading AF3** • Simple, plausible inference about events and information, using evidence from text. • Comments based on textual cues, sometimes misunderstood.	**Reading AF3** • Straightforward inference based on a single point of reference in the text. • Responses to text show meaning established at a literal level or based on personal speculation.	• I can identify facts in a newspaper article. • I can identify opinions in a newspaper article.
Phase ③ activities pages 90-92				
Read all about it! Children can identify key language and presentational features of newspapers and magazines.	• Paired activity where children identify and comment on the features of a newspaper article. • Completed photocopiable pages.	**Reading AF4** Some awareness of use of features of organisation.	**Reading AF4** A few basic features of organisation at text level identified, with little or no linked comment.	• I can identify language features of a newspaper article. • I can identify presentational features of a newspaper article.
Pronouns Children can draft a newspaper or magazine article based on a recount.	• Independent activity where children rewrite sentences of a recount in the third person. • Completed photocopiable pages.	**Reading AF5** • Some effective language choices noted. • Some familiar patterns of language identified.	**Reading AF5** A few basic features of writer's use of language identified, but with little or no comment.	• I can identify pronouns which are in the first person. • I can change the first person to the third person in a sentence.

Unit 1 ■ Recounts: newspapers/magazines

Learning outcomes	Assessment opportunity and evidence	Assessment focuses (AFs)		Success criteria
		Level 2	Level 3	
Phase ④ activities pages 92–93				
Collecting the news Children can record evidence for a newspaper article based on a range of evidence sources.	● Whole-class activity where children make notes on the news report from the interactive activity. ● Children's verbal responses and completed graphic organisers.	**Writing AF3** ● Some basic sequencing of ideas or material. ● Openings and/or closings sometimes signalled.	**Writing AF3** ● Some attempt to organise ideas with related points placed next to each other. ● Openings and closings usually signalled. ● Some attempt to sequence ideas or material logically.	● I can make notes for a newspaper article. ● I can use a graphic organiser to sequence events and information.
Writing the news Children can plan, draft and publish a newspaper article using the appropriate language and presentational features.	● Supported activity where children write a newspaper article. ● Children's completed newspaper articles.	**Writing AF2** ● Some basic purpose established. ● Some appropriate features of the given form used. ● Some attempts to adopt appropriate style.	**Writing AF2** ● Purpose established at a general level. ● Main features of selected form sometimes signalled to the reader. ● Some attempts at appropriate style, with attention to reader.	● I can write using the past tense. ● I can write in the third person. ● I can include an introductory paragraph that answers the five Ws. ● I can include a photograph with a caption. ● I can include a quote. ● I can write a headline using alliteration.

Learning outcomes	Assessment opportunity and evidence	Assessment focuses (AFs)		Success criteria
		Level 4	Level 5	
Phase ① activities pages 87–88				
My trip to London Children can organise and sequence a recount, identifying key events.	● Independent activity where children use a recount text to sequence photographs and captions in the interactive activity. ● Completed interactive activity.	**Reading AF2** ● Some relevant points identified. ● Comments supported by some generally relevant textual reference or quotation.	**Reading AF2** ● Most relevant points clearly identified, including those selected from different places in the text. ● Comments generally supported by relevant textual reference or quotation, even when points made are not always accurate.	I can sequence the key events of a recount.
Our school trip Children can write a draft recount in the correct verb tense.	● Independent activity where children draft a recount using a timeline. ● Children's draft recount timeline.	**Writing AF3** ● Ideas organised by clustering related points or by time sequence. ● Ideas are organised simply with a fitting opening and closing, sometimes linked . ● Ideas or material generally in logical sequence but overall direction of writing not always clearly signalled.	**Writing AF3** ● Material is structured clearly, with sentences organised into appropriate paragraphs. ● Development of material is effectively managed across text . ● Overall direction of the text supported by clear links between paragraphs.	● I can plan my recount using a timeline, connectives and question words. ● I can write a draft recount in the first person. ● I can use the past tense in my writing.

Unit 1 ◻ Recounts: newspapers/magazines

Learning outcomes	Assessment opportunity and evidence	Assessment focuses (AFs)		Success criteria
		Level 4	Level 5	
Phase ② activities pages 89-90				
Fact or opinion? Children can orally distinguish between factual information and opinions based on factual information.	● Independent activity where children use the recount text to identify facts and opinions. ● Completed photocopiable pages.	**Reading AF3** ● Comments make inferences based on evidence from different points in the text. ● Inferences often correct, but comments are not always rooted securely in the text or repeat narrative or content.	**Reading AF3** ● Comments develop explanation of inferred meanings drawing on evidence across the text. ● Comments make inferences and deductions based on textual evidence.	● I can find examples of facts in a text. ● I can find examples of opinions in a text.
Finding facts and opinions Children can identify and record factual information and opinions based on factual information.	● Paired activity where children identify facts and opinions in a newspaper article. ● Completed photocopiable pages.	**Reading AF3** ● Comments make inferences based on evidence from different points in the text. ● Inferences often correct, but comments are not always rooted securely in the text or repeat narrative or content.	**Reading AF3** ● Comments develop explanation of inferred meanings drawing on evidence across the text. ● Comments make inferences and deductions based on textual evidence.	● I can identify facts in a newspaper article. ● I can identify opinions in a newspaper article.
Phase ③ activities pages 90-92				
Read all about it! Children can identify key language and presentational features of newspapers and magazines.	● Paired activity where children identify and comment on the features of a newspaper article. ● Completed photocopiable pages.	**Reading AF4** ● Some structural choices identified with simple comment. ● Some basic features of organisation at text level identified.	**Reading AF4** ● Comments on structural choices show some general awareness of writer's craft. ● Various features relating to organisation at text level, including form, are clearly identified, with some explanation.	● I can identify language features of a newspaper article. ● I can identify presentational features of a newspaper article.
Pronouns Children can draft a newspaper or magazine article based on a recount.	● Independent activity where children rewrite sentences of a recount in the third person. ● Completed photocopiable pages.	**Reading AF5** ● Some basic features of writer's use of language identified. ● Simple comments on writer's choices.	**Reading AF5** ● Various features of writer's use of language identified, with some explanation. ● Comments show some awareness of the effect of writer's language choices.	● I can identify pronouns which are in the first person. ● I can change the first person to the third person in a sentence.
Phase ④ activities pages 92-93				
Collecting the news Children can record evidence for a newspaper article based on a range of evidence sources.	● Whole-class activity where children make notes on the news report from the interactive activity. ● Children's verbal responses and completed graphic organisers.	**Writing AF3** ● Ideas organised by clustering related points or by time sequence. ● Ideas are organised simply with a fitting opening and closing, sometimes linked. ● Ideas or material generally in logical sequence but overall direction of writing not always clearly signalled.	**Writing AF3** ● Material is structured clearly, with sentences organised into appropriate paragraphs. ● Development of material is effectively managed across text. ● Overall direction of the text supported by clear links between paragraphs.	● I can make notes for a newspaper article. ● I can use a graphic organiser to sequence events and information.
Writing the news Children can plan, draft and publish a newspaper article using the appropriate language and presentational features.	● Independent activity where children write a newspaper article. ● Children's completed newspaper articles.	**Writing AF2** ● Main purpose of writing is clear but not always consistently maintained. ● Main features of selected form are clear and appropriate to purpose. ● Style generally appropriate to task, though awareness of reader not always sustained.	**Writing AF2** ● Main purpose of writing is clear and consistently maintained. ● Features of selected form clearly established with some adaptation to purpose. ● Appropriate style clearly established to maintain reader's interest throughout.	● I can write using the past tense. ● I can write in the third person. ● I can include an introductory paragraph that answers the five Ws. ● I can include a photograph with a caption. ● I can include a quote. ● I can write a headline using alliteration.

Phase ①	My trip to London

NON-FICTION

Learning outcome
Children can organise and sequence a recount, identifying key events.

Success criteria
I can sequence the key events of a recount.

Setting the context
The children will need to be familiar with the main features of recount – it is in the first person, in the past tense and the first paragraph should include answers to the five questions: 'what', 'where', 'when', 'why' and 'who'. Introduce the success criteria and explain to the children that they are going to work individually to sequence a series of photographs into chronological order and match captions to the photographs. These will develop their understanding of the use of time connectives.

Assessment opportunity
Tell the children that they are going to read a recount, written by a child, about a summer holiday trip to London. Hand out the photocopiable page 'My trip to London' and ask the children to use the recount to help them to sequence the photographs on the first screen of the interactive activity 'My trip to London'. Children working at levels 2–3 will need to work with support while those at levels 4–5 will work independently. Encourage the children to consider the order of events by asking questions such as: *What did the children do first? Where did they go after that?* Next, tell them to use the second screen to sequence the captions for each photograph. Encourage children to identify the time connectives. Ask them to suggest other connectives they could use such as 'later', 'eventually', 'after' and 'once'. Assess whether children are able to identify key points in a text and whether they know how to locate the information they need.

Assessment evidence
At levels 2–3, children will be able recall and identify the most obvious events in the recount and will use this information to sequence the photographs and captions – although they may need several attempts to do this correctly. At levels 4–5, children will use relevant points from the text to sequence the events correctly and they will be able to refer back to the text to identify alternative connectives for their captions such as 'Eventually we spotted the Millennium Dome'. The activity will enable evidence to be gathered against Reading AF2.

Next steps
Support: Encourage children to revisit the text and use a highlighter to identify the key events. Help them to number them and make a list. This can then be used with the interactive resource to assist with sequencing photographs and captions.
Extension: Have more confident learners print off the photographs and write their own captions, using the recount text.

Key aspects of learning
Enquiry: Children will be learning to ask who? what? where? when? and why? when researching a news story for a written or oral report.
Information processing: Children will be identifying relevant information from a range of multi-media sources and using this as a basis for both planning and writing.

Phase ① Our school trip

Learning outcome
Children can write a draft recount in the correct verb tense.

Success criteria
- I can plan my recount using a timeline, connectives and question words.
- I can write a draft recount in the first person.
- I can use the past tense in my writing.

Setting the context
The children will need to be familiar with the main features of a recount. They will also need to have a series of five photographs from a school trip or event that all the children have participated in. The children will first work as a whole class to organise the photographs into chronological order and then individually on the photocopiable page 'Recount timeline'.

Assessment opportunity
Invite the children to organise the photographs into chronological order. (This could be a whiteboard activity.) Make notes of the time connectives that children verbally use to describe the chronology of the trip or event. Following the whole-class activity, provide children with a set of five photographs (reduced black and white photocopies are fine) and photocopiable page 'Recount timeline'. Tell the children to organise the photographs on the timeline and annotate each photograph with a caption using time connectives. Encourage children to recount the events orally before writing. While children are writing their caption sentences, discuss with them the order in which events occurred and observe whether they use time connectives to recount the event. Invite them to identify the verb in each caption and explain which tense it is written in. Can they tell you what the verb would be in the present or future tense? Discuss children's choices of connectives. Have they thought about which connectives help the reader to understand the passage of time during their recount? Record the children's verbal responses where appropriate and evaluate written work against the success criteria.

Assessment evidence
At levels 2–3, children will sequence some of the photographs in a logical way and will make some attempt to use simple time connectives in their captions. At levels 4–5, children will place the photographs into a logical sequence and their captions will use fitting time connectives. The children's verbal responses and your notes will provide evidence towards Writing AF3.

Next steps
Support: Provide children with time-connective sentence starters for each photograph if they are struggling to vary their use of connectives.
Extension: Have the children go on to write their recount, in paragraphs.

Key aspects of learning
Enquiry: Children will be learning to ask who? what? where? when? and why? when researching a news story for a written or oral report.
Information processing: Children will be identifying relevant information from a range of multi-media sources and using this as a basis for both planning and writing.

Phase ② Fact or opinion?

Learning outcome
Children can orally distinguish between factual information and opinions based on factual information.

Success criteria
- I can find examples of facts in a text.
- I can find examples of opinions in a text.

Setting the context
Children will need to have read the recount on the photocopiable page, 'My trip to London'. Recap the meaning of fact and opinion. Explain that they are going to identify facts and opinions in the text and distinguish between them.

Assessment opportunity
With the whole class, revisit the recount on the photocopiable page 'My trip to London'. Do the children think that the boy who wrote the recount enjoyed his trip to London? Remind them that this is an opinion and ask what evidence they can give you to support this opinion. Observe their verbal responses. Give each child working at levels 2–3 version 1 of the photocopiable page 'Fact or opinion?' and ask them to use it alongside the text extract to answer the questions. They could also use the interactive activity 'Fact or opinion?'. Ask children working at levels 4–5 to scan the text and locate phrases and sentences that constitute facts and opinions. They should then complete version 2 of the photocopiable page 'Fact or opinion?'. Assess the children's ability to interpret information using evidence from the text to back up their inferences.

Assessment evidence
At levels 2–3, children will be able to identify facts from the text as well as make straightforward inferences, for example, 'He enjoyed the train journey because it says "he had fun on the train, did drawings and played games"'. At levels 4–5, children will be able to identify relevant facts. They may also make inferences that are backed up by evidence from different points in the text, for example, 'George thought the underground was "too busy" and crowded. Earlier, he said he liked the other train because "there was more room"'. The completed activity will provide evidence against mainly Reading AF3 (see also Reading AF2).

Next steps
Support: Encourage children to use a highlighter to find and highlight textual evidence in the recount before answering the questions.
Extension: Ask children to add on a reflective paragraph to the end of the recount, imagining they were George, to say what their opinion was of the day including likes and dislikes, impressions of London and the places and things he saw.

Key aspects of learning
Reasoning: Children will develop judgements on what is 'fact' and what is 'opinion' based on available evidence.

Phase ② Finding facts and opinions

Learning outcome
Children can identify and record factual information and opinions based on factual information.

Success criteria
● I can identity facts in a newspaper article.
● I can identify opinions in a newspaper article.

Setting the context
Children will need to have had prior experience of identifying fact and opinion. Provide children with a number of carefully selected current newspaper articles which include several facts and opinions. The children will need to read the articles with a partner and then select one that interests them to work on.

Assessment opportunity
Ask the children to work in pairs to read the newspaper article they have chosen again and then record examples of facts and opinions on paper. Next ask them to identify quotes. *Do the quotes represent factual information or are they the thoughts of that person?* Can they explain what a different person may say about the same issue? Encourage the children to express their viewpoints and assess their ability to make plausible deductions.

Assessment evidence
At levels 2–3, children will be able to make simple inferences regarding facts and opinions although there may be some misunderstanding. At levels 4–5, children will be able to deduce whether quotes from the text are facts or opinions and will begin to express their own viewpoints drawing on evidence from the text. This activity will enable you to gather evidence against Reading AF3.

Next steps
Support: Read the newspaper articles with children and ask leading questions to help direct them to specific information in the texts: *Can you find a caption for the photograph? Who wrote this article? What does the headline tell you?*
Extension: Encourage children to write from their own viewpoints as a result of reading the article.

Key aspects of learning
Information processing: Children will be identifying relevant information from a range of multi-media sources and using this as a basis for both planning and writing.
Reasoning: Children will develop judgements on what is 'fact' and what is 'opinion' based on available evidence.

Phase ③ Read all about it!

Learning outcome
Children can identify key language and presentational features of newspapers and magazines.

Success criteria
● I can identify language features of a newspaper article.
● I can identify presentational features of a newspaper article.

Setting the context
Children will need to be familiar with the main features of newspaper articles. Present children with a number of carefully selected newspaper articles about a range of issues (such as world news, local news or sport). Ask them to work in pairs to read through several of the articles and to choose the one they want to study in detail.

Assessment opportunity
Give all the children the photocopiable page 'Features of a newspaper article', which

■SCHOLASTIC

they can use alongside their chosen report to identify examples of all the different features. Can they identify and comment on the structural and organisational features of this particular text type? Can they point out different features, such as introductory paragraphs? Can they say why a headline is effective? Once they have completed the activity, invite the children to discuss how the newspaper reports are written: in the past tense, in the third person and use of quotations.

Assessment evidence
At levels 2–3, children will identify some of the organisational features of a newspaper report, for example, headlines, bylines, captions, columns and photographs. At levels 4–5, children will be able to comment further on the features, for example, how a particular headline attracts the reader's interest. This activity enables evidence to be gathered against Reading AF4.

Next steps
Support: Cut up copies of the newspaper report into the different sections and invite children to identify which features each cut-out part represents.
Extension: Children can compare two different reports about the same event and give their opinion as to which is the most interesting or informative and explain why.

Key aspects of learning
Information processing: Children will be identifying relevant information from a range of multi-media sources and using this as a basis for both planning and writing.
Communication: Children will develop their ability to discuss the content and presentation of the news reports they are reading and writing. They will often work collaboratively in pairs and groups. They will communicate outcomes orally, in writing and through ICT.

Phase ③ Pronouns

Learning outcome
Children can draft a newspaper or magazine article based on a recount.

Success criteria
● I can identify pronouns which are in the first person.
● I can change the first person to the third person in a sentence.

Setting the context
In this activity, children will use extracts from the recount of the trip to London on the photocopiable page 'Pronouns' to identify first person pronouns. They will need to know that the recount was written by the person who experienced it and that it is written in the first person. Children will also need to know the pronouns that relate to the first person (I, me, my, mine, our, we, us). Recap if necessary the fact that in a newspaper recount, the author is reporting information or the experiences of other people. These are written using third-person pronouns (he, she, they, them, theirs, his, hers).

Assessment opportunity
Give all the children the photocopiable page 'Pronouns' and ask them to highlight all the examples of first person pronouns in the text. They should then rewrite these sentences in the third person. As children are highlighting the first person pronouns, ask them to tell you the third person equivalent. Can they explain why the author has used first person pronouns in the recount? Do they understand the difference between personal and possessive pronouns (me/my; you/your)? Observe how many of the pronouns the children can identify and change successfully. This may also be an opportunity to assess handwriting for children working at levels 2–3.

Assessment evidence
At levels 2–3, children will identify some pronouns in the text. At levels 4–5, children may comment that the text is written in the first person and may explain why

NON-FICTION

authors' use of pronouns varies according to the type of recount being written. This activity will provide evidence against Reading AF5.

Next steps
Support: Provide cards with each pronoun on for children to search for if they are struggling to identify pronouns. Write the third person equivalent on the reverse. Children can then use these cards to change the first person into the third person.
Extension: Ask children to rewrite the personal recount as a newspaper article. Highlight the need to vary the use of the pronoun 'he' and the use of the name.

Key aspects of learning
Communication: Children will develop their ability to discuss the content and presentation of the news reports they are reading and writing.

Phase ④ Collecting the news

Learning outcome
Children can record evidence for a newspaper article based on a range of evidence sources.

Success criteria
● I can make notes for a newspaper article.
● I can use a graphic organiser to sequence events and information.

Setting the context
Children will need to be familiar with features of newspaper reports. Tell the children that they are going to watch a news 'video' and that they must take notes on the events. They will then use an interactive activity in conjunction with the photocopiable page 'Graphic organiser' to assist them in making notes in preparation for writing their own newspaper report.

Assessment opportunity
Read the information in the interactive activity 'Trapped terrier's amazing rescue' as a whole class and then encourage the children to explain the order in which the events occurred. As the children recount the events, observe their use of time connectives used to link the events ('soon after', 'immediately' and so on). Invite them to explain what they will include in the opening paragraph (refer them to the question-word prompts on the photocopiable page 'Graphic organiser'). The interactive activity includes a quote from an eyewitness. Invite children to suggest how they will report people's opinions about the event.

Assessment evidence
At levels 2–3, children's notes will indicate basic sequencing of material or grouping of related information. At levels 4–5, children's notes will be organised into a logical sequence. Use the completed photocopiable sheets and children's verbal responses as evidence against Writing AF3.

Next steps
Support: Re-watch the interactive news video with the children, stopping at intervals to record each event that occurs as a sentence on their whiteboards.
Extension: Children can use BBC *Newsround* video footage as material for writing further newspaper articles.

Key aspects of learning
Enquiry: Children will be learning to ask who? what? where? when? and why? when researching a news story for a written or oral report.
Information processing: Children will be identifying relevant information from a range of multi-media sources and using this as a basis for both planning and writing.
Communication: Children will develop their ability to discuss the content and presentation of the news reports they are reading and writing. They will often work collaboratively in pairs and groups. They will communicate outcomes orally, in writing and through ICT.

NON-FICTION

Phase ④ Writing the news

Success criteria
- I can write using the past tense.
- I can write in the third person.
- I can include an introductory paragraph that answers the five Ws.
- I can include a photograph with a caption.
- I can include a quote.
- I can write a headline using alliteration.

Setting the context
The children will need to have completed the previous activity and will use their completed graphic organisers to write a newspaper report about the event from the interactive activity 'Trapped terrier's amazing rescue'. They will need to use all the features of a newspaper article in their writing to ensure that they are familiar with these and recap as necessary. Display the success criteria for the children to refer to during the activity.

Assessment opportunity
Give the children their completed graphic organisers from the previous activity and the photocopiable page 'Newspaper article'. Ask them to write their newspaper reports based on the topic from the interactive activity 'Trapped terrier's amazing rescue'. Allow plenty of time for this. Support children working at levels 2-3 and model how to use the success criteria to refine their work. Assess how well children develop the purpose of their writing and whether they include the features of the genre. Once they have completed the activity, ask pairs of children to swap their newspaper articles and carry out peer assessment using the photocopiable page 'Newspaper article review'. You can also mark some children's writing against the success criteria.

Assessment evidence
At levels 2-3, children will include some features of newspaper reports, such as headline, byline, photographs and captions in their writing. They will also have made an attempt to adopt the style of newspaper reports. At levels 4-5, children will use appropriately all the features of newspaper reports such as an attention-grabbing headline and so on. Their opening paragraph will establish a clear purpose for their writing. This activity will provide evidence against mainly Writing AF2 (see also all the other Writing AFs).

Next steps
Support: Have the children write six sentences to answer the questions 'who', 'what', 'where' and 'when'. These six sentences can then be connected and drawn together to form the first paragraph of a news report.
Extension: Children could choose different video footage from BBC *Newsround* to report on and create a class newspaper using an ICT publishing program.

Key aspects of learning
Enquiry: Children will be learning to ask who? what? where? when? and why? when researching a news story for a written or oral report.
Information processing: Children will be identifying relevant information from a range of multi-media sources and using this as a basis for both planning and writing.
Communication: Children will develop their ability to discuss the content and presentation of the news reports they are reading and writing. They will often work collaboratively in pairs and groups. They will communicate outcomes orally, in writing and through ICT.

Periodic assessment

Reading

Learning outcome
Children can record evidence for a newspaper article based on a range of evidence sources.

Success criteria
I can use a graphic organiser to sequence events and information.

Setting the context
The children are going to gather information for writing a report, referring to a news reporter's notebook. They should imagine that they are the reporter, who has returned to the office to write their report. They will complete a graphic organiser using the information available in preparation for writing their newspaper recount.

Assessment opportunity
Give each child a copy of the photocopiable page 'Non-fiction 1 Reading assessment text' and ask them to use the journalist's notes to complete the graphic organiser on the photocopiable page 'Non-fiction 1 Reading assessment'. Ask open questions before they complete their graphic organisers to identify how well children are able to scan the notes to locate the relevant information. Can they think of a suitable caption for the photograph?

Assessment evidence:
At levels 2–3, children will make notes on the most obvious points from the text. They will also make basic inferences from the text, such as 'We know that houses were ruined because it says "homes were destroyed".' At levels 4–5, children will make inferences based on evidence from different points in the text , for example, 'We know it was dangerous in Texas after Hurricane Ike struck because it says "people have been told to stay off the streets" and later on it says "don't venture out unless you absolutely have to".' They will also sequence events logically. This activity will provide evidence against Reading AF2 and AF3. Use this activity and evidence gathered throughout this unit to help you judge children's overall level in Reading.

Periodic assessment

Writing

Learning outcome
Children can plan, draft and publish a newspaper article using the appropriate language and presentational features.

Success criteria
- I can write using the past tense.
- I can write a newspaper report in the third person.
- I have included an introductory paragraph that answers the five Ws.
- I have included a quote in my newspaper report.
- I have included a photograph with a caption.
- I can write a headline using alliteration.

Setting the context
This activity assumes the children have completed the Periodic Reading assessment on page 94. The children will also need to have experience in using an ICT publishing program. Using their completed graphic organisers and the photograph of the hurricane from the photocopiable page 'Non-fiction 1 Reading assessment text', the children will write a newspaper report incorporating all the organisational and language features of a newspaper recount. Ensure the success criteria are clearly displayed for the children to refer to during the activity.

Assessment opportunity
Check whether children can write consistently in the past tense, in the third person and can use speech marks to record quotes from eyewitnesses. Have they chosen an appropriate headline for the article and written it in bold, large font? Have they included all the answers to the five questions in their first paragraph? Have they included a photograph with a caption? Children can type, edit and present their news reports using a suitable ICT publishing program. Encourage the children to refer to the success criteria to refine their work.

Assessment evidence
This activity will assess how well children are able to structure their writing, organise it into paragraphs and use the features of a specific genre. This activity can also be used to gather evidence against all the Writing AFs. Use this activity along with other samples of children's completed work to assess their current level in Writing.

Name _____ Date _____

Fact or opinion? (1)

◼ Answer the questions below to identify the facts from the opinions.

FACTS

1. How many objects in the exhibition were excavated from Tutankhamun's tomb?

_____ objects in the exhibition were excavated from Tutankhamun's tomb.

2. Where does the name Big Ben come from?

_____

3. Who discovered Tutankhamun's tomb?

_____

4. When was the tomb discovered?

_____

OPINIONS

5. What did George think of the train journey? Why?

He thought the train journey was _____ because

_____

6. What did he think of the Underground? Why?

_____

7. What did George think of the exhibition? Why?

_____

8. What did George think about the sarcophagus not being there? Why?

_____

Red
Amber
Green

I can find examples of facts in a text. ☐

I can find examples of opinions in a text. ☐

Name	Date

Graphic organiser

◼ Use the graphic organiser below to plan your newspaper article.

My chosen headline: _____

WHO	WHAT
_____	_____
_____	_____
_____	_____

WHY	WHEN
_____	_____
_____	_____
_____	_____

Photo caption:

_____

_____

_____

_____

_____

WHERE

_____

_____

_____

Quote: _____

_____

Red
Amber
Green

I can make notes for a newspaper report. ⬜

I can use a graphic organiser to sequence events and information. ⬜

NON-FICTION

NON-FICTION
UNIT 2 Information texts

Literacy objectives

Speak and listen for a wide range of purposes in different contexts
Strand 3 Group discussion and interaction
- Take different roles in groups and use the language appropriate to them, including the roles of leader, reporter, scribe and mentor.

Read and write for a range of purposes on paper and on screen
Strand 7 Understanding and interpreting texts
- Deduce characters' reasons for behaviour from their actions and explain how ideas are developed in non-fiction texts.

Strand 8 Engaging with and responding to texts
- Interrogate texts to deepen and clarify understanding and response.

Strand 9 Creating and shaping texts
- Develop and refine ideas in writing using planning and problem-solving strategies.
- Summarise and shape material and ideas from different sources to write convincing and informative non-narrative texts.
- Choose and combine words, images and other features for particular effects.

Strand 10 Text structure and organisation
- Organise text into paragraphs to distinguish between different information, events or processes.
- Use adverbs and conjunctions to establish cohesion within paragraphs.

Strand 11 Sentence structure and punctuation
- Clarify meaning and point of view by using varied sentence structure (phrases, clauses and adverbials).

Strand 12 Presentation
- Use word-processing packages to present written work and continue to increase speed and accuracy in typing.

Key aspects of learning

Creative thinking
- Children will generate and extend imaginative ideas to create a text. They will suggest hypotheses, responding imaginatively through drama and talk, and respond to problems to create a written outcome.

Self-awareness
- Children will discuss and reflect on their personal responses to the texts.

Evaluation
- Children will present information orally, diagrammatically and in writing. They will discuss success criteria, give feedback to others and judge the effectiveness of their own work.

Communication
- Children will often work collaboratively in pairs and groups. They will communicate outcomes orally, in writing and using other modes and media where appropriate.

Assessment focuses

Reading
AF2 (*understand, describe, select or retrieve information, events or ideas from texts and use quotation and reference to text*).
AF4 (*identify and comment on the structure and organisation of texts, including grammatical and presentational features at text level*).

Writing
AF2 (*produce texts which are appropriate to task, reader and purpose*).
AF3 (*organise and present whole texts effectively, sequencing and structuring information, ideas and events*).
AF4 (*construct paragraphs and use cohesion within and between paragraphs*).
AF7 (*select appropriate and effective vocabulary*).

Speaking and listening
Group discussion and interaction (take on different roles and take turns).

Resources

Phase 1 activities
Interactive activity, 'Alphabetical ordering'
Photocopiable page, 'Glossary and dictionary definitions'
Photocopiable page, 'Information book: feature checklist'
Phase 2 activities
Photocopiable page, 'Information text spidergram'
Photocopiable page, 'Research notes'
Periodic assessment
Photocopiable page, 'Non-fiction 2 Reading assessment text'
Photocopiable page, 'Non-fiction 2 Reading assessment'
Photocopiable page, 'Non-fiction 2 Writing assessment'

Unit 2 ▢ Information texts

Learning outcomes	Assessment opportunity and evidence	Assessment focuses (AFs)		Success criteria
		Level 2	Level 3	
Phase ① activities pages 103-105				
Alphabetical ordering Children can use glossaries and dictionaries to aid understanding of non-fiction texts.	● Independent activity where children sequence glossary entries in the interactive activity. ● Completed interactive activity.	**Reading AF4** Some awareness of use of features of organisation.	**Reading AF4** A few basic features of organisation at text level identified, with little or no linked comment.	I can arrange words in alphabetical order.
Dictionary or glossary? Children can use glossaries and dictionaries to aid understanding of non-fiction texts.	● Paired/group activity where children read and compare glossary and dictionary entries. ● Children's oral responses.	**Reading AF4** Some awareness of use of features of organisation.	**Reading AF4** A few basic features of organisation at text level identified, with little or no linked comment.	● I can identify a glossary entry. ● I can identify a dictionary entry. ● I can compare a glossary definition with a dictionary definition.
Information books Children can understand the features of information books.	● Independent activity where children read information books to identify features of the text type. ● Completed photocopiable pages and children's oral responses.	**Reading AF4** Some awareness of use of features of organisation.	**Reading AF4** A few basic features of organisation at text level identified, with little or no linked comment.	I can identify the features of different information books.
Phase ② activities pages 105-106				
Get planning! Children can make notes as an aid to planning their research.	● Group activity where children brainstorm for research. ● Children's oral contributions and completed spidergrams.	**Writing AF3** ● Some basic sequencing of ideas or material. ● Openings and/or closings sometimes signalled.	**Writing AF3** ● Some attempt to organise ideas with related points placed next to each other. ● Openings and closings usually signalled. ● Some attempt to sequence ideas or material logically.	● I can use a spidergram to plan my research. ● I know where to look to find the information I need.
Take note! Children can scan texts and make notes in preparation for writing.	● Group activity where children carry out research about dinosaurs. ● Children's notes and oral responses.	**Reading AF2** ● Some specific, straightforward information recalled. ● Generally clear idea of where to look for information.	**Reading AF2** ● Simple, most obvious points identified though there may also be some misunderstanding. ● Some comments include quotations from or references to text, but not always relevant.	● I can use an internet search engine to find information. ● I can scan a non-fiction text to find information. ● I can make notes.
Phase ③ activities pages 107-108				
Poster planning Children can work cooperatively to produce a plan for an informative text.	● Group activity where children plan an information poster. ● Children's planned layouts of their posters.	**Writing AF3** ● Some basic sequencing of ideas or material. ● Openings and/or closings sometimes signalled.	**Writing AF3** ● Some attempt to organise ideas with related points placed next to each other. ● Openings and closings usually signalled. ● Some attempt to sequence ideas or material logically.	● I can plan the layout of an information poster. ● I can work sensibly in a group, putting forward ideas and listening to the ideas of others. ● I can use a checklist to make sure the poster is well planned.

Unit 2 ⬜ Information texts

Learning outcomes	Assessment opportunity and evidence	Assessment focuses (AFs)		Success criteria
		Level 2	**Level 3**	
Writing an information text Children can use their notes and plans to produce an information text including all the features of the text type.	● Independent activity where children draft, edit and publish an information text. ● Group presentation. ● Children's individual written contributions, the group presentation and self-assessment.	**Writing AF2** ● Some basic purpose established. ● Some appropriate features of the given form used. ● Some attempts to adopt appropriate style.	**Writing AF2** ● Purpose established at a general level. ● Main features of selected form sometimes signalled to the reader. ● Some attempts at appropriate style, with attention to reader.	● I can use my notes to write a paragraph. ● I can choose a subheading for my paragraph. ● I have written in the past tense because this is historical information. ● I can write using the third person. ● I can highlight the key words in my writing which are listed in the glossary. ● I can use large, bold font for headings and sub-headings. ● I can include a labelled diagram. ● I can include a glossary.

Learning outcomes	Assessment opportunity and evidence	Assessment focuses (AFs)		Success criteria
		Level 4	**Level 5**	
Phase ① activities pages 103–105				
Alphabetical ordering Children can use glossaries and dictionaries to aid understanding of non-fiction texts.	● Independent activity where children sequence glossary entries in the interactive activity. ● Completed interactive activity.	**Reading AF4** ● Some structural choices identified with simple comment. ● Some basic features of organisation at text level identified.	**Reading AF4** ● Comments on structural choices show some general awareness of writer's craft. ● Various features relating to organisation at text level, including form, are clearly identified, with some explanation.	I can arrange words in alphabetical order.
Dictionary or glossary? Children can use glossaries and dictionaries to aid understanding of non-fiction texts.	● Paired/group activity where children read and compare glossary and dictionary entries. ● Children's oral responses.	**Reading AF4** ● Some structural choices identified with simple comment. ● Some basic features of organisation at text level identified.	**Reading AF4** ● Comments on structural choices show some general awareness of writer's craft. ● Various features relating to organisation at text level, including form, are clearly identified, with some explanation.	● I can identify a glossary entry. ● I can identify a dictionary entry. ● I can compare a glossary definition with a dictionary definition.
Information books Children can understand the features of information books.	● Independent activity where children read information books to identify features of the text type. ● Completed photocopiable pages and children's oral responses.	**Reading AF4** ● Some structural choices identified with simple comment. ● Some basic features of organisation at text level identified.	**Reading AF4** ● Comment on structural choices show some general awareness of writer's craft. ● Various features relating to organisation at text level, including form, are clearly identified.	I can identify the features of different information books.

Unit 2 ☐ Information texts

Learning outcomes	Assessment opportunity and evidence	Assessment focuses (AFs)		Success criteria
		Level 4	Level 5	
Phase ② activities pages 105–106				
Get planning! Children can make notes as an aid to planning their research.	● Group activity where children brainstorm for research. ● Children's oral contributions and completed spidergrams.	**Writing AF3** ● Ideas organised by clustering related points or by time sequence. ● Ideas are organised simply with a fitting opening and closing, sometimes linked. ● Ideas or material generally in logical sequence but overall direction of writing not always clearly signalled.	**Writing AF3** ● Material is structured clearly, with sentences organised into appropriate paragraphs. ● Development of material is effectively managed across text. ● Overall direction of the text supported by clear links between paragraphs.	● I can use a spidergram to plan my research. ● I know where to look to find the information I need.
Take note! Children can scan texts and make notes in preparation for writing.	● Group activity where children carry out research about dinosaurs. ● Children's notes and oral responses.	**Reading AF2** ● Some relevant points identified. ● Comments supported by some generally relevant textual reference or quotation.	**Reading AF2** ● Most relevant points clearly identified, including those selected from different places in the text. ● Comments generally supported by relevant textual reference or quotation, even when points made are not always accurate.	● I can use an internet search engine to find information. ● I can scan a non-fiction text to find information. ● I can make notes.
Phase ③ activities pages 107–108				
Poster planning Children can work cooperatively to produce a plan for an informative text.	● Group activity where children plan an information poster. ● Children's planned layouts of their posters.	**Writing AF3** ● Ideas organised by clustering related points or by time sequence. ● Ideas are organised simply with a fitting opening and closing, sometimes linked.	**Writing AF3** ● Material is structured clearly, with sentences organised into appropriate paragraphs. ● Development of material is effectively managed across text. ● Overall direction of the text supported by clear links between paragraphs.	● I can plan the layout of an information poster. ● I can work sensibly in a group, putting forward ideas and listening to the ideas of others. ● I can use a checklist to make sure the poster is well planned.
Writing an information text Children can use their notes and plans to produce an information text including all the features of the text type.	● Independent activity where children draft, edit and publish an information text. ● Group presentation. ● Children's individual written contributions, the group presentation and self-assessment.	**Writing AF2** ● Main purpose of writing is clear but not always consistently maintained ● Main features of selected form are clear and appropriate to purpose. ● Style generally appropriate to task, though awareness of reader not always sustained.	**Writing AF2** ● Main purpose of writing is clear and consistently maintained. ● Features of selected form clearly established with some adaptation to purpose. ● Appropriate style clearly established to maintain reader's interest throughout.	● I can use my notes to write a paragraph. ● I can choose a subheading for my paragraph. ● I have written in the past tense because this is historical information. ● I can write using the third person. ● I can highlight the key words in my writing which are listed in the glossary. ● I can use large, bold font for headings and sub-headings. ● I can include a labelled diagram. ● I can include a glossary.

Phase ① Alphabetical ordering

Learning outcome
Children can use glossaries and dictionaries to aid understanding of non-fiction texts.

Success criteria
I can arrange words in alphabetical order.

Setting the context
It is important for the children to practise sorting information alphabetically in order to be able to use information texts effectively (glossaries, dictionaries, encyclopedias and telephone directories, for instance). The children will need to have experienced alphabetically ordering words that start with the same letter(s).

Assessment opportunity
Explain to the children how to use the interactive activity 'Alphabetical ordering'. The first screen requires the children to sort by the first letter, the second screen by the second letter, third by third letter and fourth by fourth letter. As children are sequencing the words, invite them to tell you their rationale for doing so. Assess whether children are able to recognise and comment on organisational features.

Assessment evidence
At levels 2–3, children will organise words alphabetically up to the second and third letters but will make little comment regarding organisation of the text. At levels 4–5, children will sequence words accurately up to the fourth and fifth letters and they will explain why sections of a glossary should be structured alphabetically. This activity provides evidence against Reading AF4 (see also Reading AF2).

Next steps
Support: Where children are struggling to sort words by second or third letter for example, produce the words cut up on card. Use a single colour highlighter to highlight the letter by which the words are to be ordered. Then use an alphabet strip to help the children organise the words into the correct order.
Extension: Encourage children to create alphabetically-organised glossaries for display purposes related to ongoing topics in foundation subjects.

Key aspects of learning
Evaluation: Children will present information orally, diagrammatically and in writing. They will discuss success criteria, give feedback to others and judge the effectiveness of their own work.

Phase ① Dictionary or glossary?

Learning outcome
Children can use glossaries and dictionaries to aid understanding of non-fiction texts.

Success criteria
● I can identify a glossary entry.
● I can identify a dictionary entry.
● I can compare a glossary definition with a dictionary definition.

Setting the context
Establish the differences between dictionaries and glossaries. A dictionary is a reference book that contains the meanings of the words in a language in alphabetical order. A glossary is a section at the back of a reference book that lists words relating to the book's subject and their meanings, also in alphabetical order.

Assessment opportunity
Encourage the children to look up specific words in class dictionaries (a variety of different editions would be useful) and in glossaries of information books. Give the children the photocopiable page 'Glossary and dictionary definitions' on which to

NON-FICTION

record the information that each entry provides. At the end, ask them to sum up the differences between the glossary and the dictionary entries. *When would you use a dictionary to search for a word? When would you use a glossary?* Ask the children to work in pairs or small groups to compare the information they have found. These groups then report back to the class. Use the oral contributions to draw a class conclusion about the uses of the different types of information provided. Observe whether the children are able to locate word entries and can make comparisons between the organisational features of a dictionary and a glossary.

Assessment evidence
At levels 2–3, children may make limited statements on the structure of the texts, for example, 'It tells you what a word means.' At levels 4–5, children will expand their comments on the structure of the texts by explaining when each type of entry would be useful and why they might need the information. This activity provides evidence against Reading AF4 (see also Reading AF2).

Next steps
Support: Provide dictionaries appropriate to ability level. Have the children practise looking up words using headwords. Revisit word types and give examples of their use.
Extension: For dictionary practice, play word chains. Provide children with a starter word, for example, 'dinosaur'. They look up the word, find specific information and record it. They then look up a key word contained in the definition such as 'reptile' or 'extinct'. Continue the game for about ten words and see which word the children end up with!

Key aspects of learning
Self-awareness: Children will discuss and reflect on their personal responses to the texts.
Evaluation: Children will present information orally, diagrammatically and in writing. They will discuss success criteria, give feedback to others and judge the effectiveness of their own work.

Phase ① Information books

Learning outcome
Children can understand the features of information books.

Success criteria
I can identify the features of different information books.

Setting the context
Ensure that children are comfortable with the idea of an information book. Visit the school library and discuss different examples of information books and their specific features. This may involve providing an example of an entry ('You can find out about fossils on page 24') or a comment on the presentation ('I liked the font for the headings because I could find what I was looking for easily').

Assessment opportunity
Ask the children to select information books from the school library that interest them to carry out an information book feature check using photocopiable page 'Information book: feature checklist'. Ask them to locate and identify examples of the features listed on the sheet and make comments. Observe how the children 'navigate' their way around the books they choose. Can they find and use the index and contents pages appropriately and effectively? Do they understand how to identify words in the glossary? Do they know what a bibliography is?

Assessment evidence
At levels 2–3, children will be able to recognise some of the organisational features in the text. At levels 4–5, children will comment on most of the structural and organisational features. This activity provides evidence towards Reading AF4.

Next steps
Support: Follow up work on features of non-fiction books in a guided reading session.
Extension: Children could choose two books on the same subject and compare the features to assess which book is the most useful, appealing or easy to use.

Key aspects of learning
Self-awareness: Children will discuss and reflect on their personal responses to the texts.

Phase ② Get planning!

Learning outcome
Children can make notes as an aid to planning their research.

Success criteria
- I can use a spidergram to plan my research.
- I know where to look to find the information I need.

Setting the context
Explain to the children that they will be carrying out research about dinosaurs (or another topic if preferred – adapt photocopiable sheets accordingly) using a variety of sources to create an 'information text' incorporating features such as headings, subheadings, glossary of terms and diagrams with captions. They will work in groups through the process of planning, drafting, editing and final publication in order to create a poster which demonstrates use of all the features. Some of their research will be carried out at home.

Assessment opportunity
Put children into groups of five and number them one to five. (If there is a group of six, allocate two children the same number.) Give each group the photocopiable page 'Information text spidergram'. For the first task, children work in their home groups to brainstorm what they would like to find out about each of the five areas on the sheet. Ask them to devise questions they would like to research the answers to and record them on the sheet. Observe children as they carry out their planning. Can they make suggestions and share ideas? How well do they formulate their ideas into specific questions? Make notes on the children's oral contributions and their ability to sequence and organise their ideas during the group planning session.

Assessment evidence
At levels 2–3, children may attempt to place some related ideas next to each other on the spidergram. At level 4–5, children will organise their spidergrams by clustering related questions. The completed spidergrams will provide evidence against Writing AF3.

Next steps
Support: Work with children to take their ideas and demonstrate how to formulate a specific question that can be used for research.
Extension: Children may add onto their planning sheets where and how they will locate the information required.

Key aspects of learning
Evaluation: Children will present information orally, diagrammatically and in writing. They will discuss success criteria, give feedback to others and judge the effectiveness of their own work.
Communication: Children will often work collaboratively in pairs and groups. They will communicate outcomes orally, in writing and using other modes and media where appropriate.

NON-FICTION

NON-FICTION

Phase ② Take note!

Success criteria
● I can use an internet search engine to find information.
● I can scan a non-fiction text to find information.
● I can make notes.

Setting the context
Once the home groups have carried out their planning and each child has a copy of the group spidergram from the previous activity, re-organise the groups into expert groups so that all the 'ones' are together, all the 'twos' are together, and so on. Assign one of the five topics of research to each numbered group. For example, Expert Group One will research fossils. The groups bring together all the questions formed during the planning session and decide who is going to research each question, ensuring material is not duplicated. Give each child the photocopiable page 'Research notes'.

Assessment opportunity
Ask the expert groups to carry out research using specific internet sites and information texts, making notes which answer their research questions on the sheet. Then bring the class back together so the children can share the information they have found. A useful dinosaur website to direct children to is www.enchantedlearning.com/subjects/dinosaurs. Ask children to tell you what they are trying to find out. Focus on ensuring they can be specific about the information they are looking for. Can they tell you what key words they will use to look up information in contents pages, indexes and on internet searches? How will they decide which information is useful and which they will ignore? Assess whether children can scan texts to identify relevant information. It is an area that should be revisited and reviewed regularly as scanning and note-taking are important skills that require development throughout KS2.

Assessment evidence
At levels 2–3, children will be able to retrieve simple information from the text. At levels 4–5, children's notes will generally be supported by relevant quotes. The completed sheets will allow evidence to be collected against Reading AF2.

Next steps
Support: Provide children with a specific internet page or book page which contains the answer to their question to reduce the amount of scanning required to locate the information.
Extension: As children demonstrate an ability to carry out effective research, widen the range of information sources available to them. Demonstrate how to scan information to locate what they need and demonstrate how to be selective in choosing the information they record.

Key aspects of learning
Self-awareness: Children will discuss and reflect on their personal responses to the texts.
Evaluation: Children will present information orally, diagrammatically and in writing. They will discuss success criteria, give feedback to others and judge the effectiveness of their own work.
Communication: Children will often work collaboratively in pairs and groups. They will communicate outcomes orally, in writing and using other modes and media where appropriate.

Phase ③ Poster planning

Learning outcome
Children can work co-operatively to produce a plan for an informative text.

Success criteria
● I can plan the layout of an information poster.
● I can work sensibly in a group, putting forward ideas and listening to the ideas of others.
● I use a checklist to make sure the poster is well planned.

Setting the context
Following the completion of the expert group research and information sharing in the previous activity, the children return to their home groups, armed with the information they have found about their specific area of research. The groups now gather together the information they have collected and decide how they are going to present the information as an information poster.

Assessment opportunity
Give each group a large sheet of sugar paper as the background. Ask them to write down and sketch, on rough paper, what and where they will place the information they are presenting and who is to produce each piece (heading, glossary of terms used, labelled diagrams, photos, paragraphs of notes with subheadings and so on). Each group must ensure everybody has a written contribution to make. Children may use the photocopiable page 'Information book: feature checklist' to help with their planning, but not all features will be essential for their poster. For effective assessment of this activity, select a number of children to target for observation. Assess whether children are able to organise and present their writing. You can also assess how well children work together in a group situation. Do they take on lead roles? Do they listen to the contributions of others and take on board their ideas? How well do they assimilate the contributions of others into the plan?

Assessment evidence
At levels 2–3, children will organise some of their written ideas appropriately with some attempts made to create a logical sequence. At levels 4–5, children's posters will generally be organised in a logical way. This activity will provide evidence against Writing AF3.

Next steps
Support: Use an adult to support children who have difficulty with contributing their ideas and information and direct turn-taking.
Extension: Children create bullet point summaries of what is to be included for each item using their research planning notes.

Key aspects of learning
Creative thinking: Children will generate and extend imaginative ideas to create a text. They will suggest hypotheses, responding imaginatively through talk, and respond to problems to create a written outcome.
Self-awareness: Children will discuss and reflect on their personal responses to the texts.
Evaluation: Children will present information orally, diagrammatically and in writing. They will discuss success criteria, give feedback to others and judge the effectiveness of their own work.
Communication: Children will often work collaboratively in pairs and groups. They will communicate outcomes orally, in writing and using other modes and media where appropriate.

NON-FICTION

Phase ③ Writing an information text

Learning outcome
Children can use their notes and plans to produce an information text including all the features of the text type.

Success criteria
● I can use my notes to write a paragraph.
● I can choose a subheading for my paragraph.
● I have written in the past tense because this is historical information.
● I can write using the third person.
● I can highlight the key words in my writing which are listed in the glossary.
● I can use a large, bold font for headings and subheadings.
● I can include a labelled diagram.
● I can include a glossary.

Setting the context
Tell the children that they will work individually to write their contribution to the collaborative group information poster or alternatively a Big Book. They should write at least one paragraph in the correct tense (past tense in this instance although information texts are usually written in the present tense) and in the third person. They should use headings, subheadings and write words to be included in a glossary in bold font. Children will also need to be confident in using an ICT word-processing program. Display the success criteria so that children can refer to it during the activity.

Assessment opportunity
Tell the children to write their draft by hand, based on their notes, and then to type up, edit and publish the final piece using an ICT word-processing program. Next, ask them to combine their individual contributions to create an information poster. Invite some children from each group to explain their contribution to the information poster. Can they describe the content of their writing? Recap with them the process of deciding what they wished to research, the questions they posed and how they researched to find the necessary information. Can they explain how they formed sentences from the notes and bullet points? Can they explain how their piece of work fits in with the rest of the group's contributions? Have the children evaluate their work against the success criteria. Assess how well children understand the purpose of their writing and whether they can clearly adopt the features of the form.

Assessment evidence
At levels 2-3, children's writing will indicate some features of information texts listed in the success criteria. At levels 4-5, children's posters will clearly show all the main features of the writing form and these will be used appropriately and purposely. This activity will provide evidence against Writing AF2.

Next steps
Support: Work with these children to help them to expand their notes into full sentences.
Extension: Provide opportunities for children to repeat the skills learned through cross-curricular work. For example, when learning about World War II children can plan and produce an information poster using the same planning and research techniques.

Key aspects of learning
Creative thinking: Children will generate and extend imaginative ideas to create a text. They will suggest hypotheses, responding imaginatively through drama and talk, and respond to problems to create a written outcome.
Communication: Children will often work collaboratively in pairs and groups. They will communicate outcomes orally, in writing and using other modes and media where appropriate.

Periodic assessment

Reading

Learning outcome Children can understand the features of information books.	

Success criteria
● I can use an information text to identify facts.
● I can find features of organisation in an information text.

Setting the context
Give the children an information text about dinosaurs. They will use the text to identify organisational features, answer questions and locate information.

Assessment opportunity
Give each child the photocopiable page 'Non-fiction 2 Reading assessment text'. Invite them to skim-read the text to get an overall impression of what the text is about before scanning the text for the specific information they need to answer the questions from the photocopiable page 'Non-fiction 2 Reading assessment'. Children should identify key words in the questions to use when scanning for information. They will also use their knowledge of the features of information texts to answer a number of the questions.

Assessment evidence
Children will identify organisational features in the text and identify relevant points from specific locations. The activity gathers evidence against Reading AF2 and AF4. Use this activity and the children's work from the rest of this unit to make a level judgement regarding their overall progress in Reading.

Writing

Learning outcome Children can develop notes into paragraphs of written text using the features of information texts.	

Success criteria
● I can use notes to write two paragraphs of information text.
● I can use headings and subheadings.
● I can highlight technical vocabulary in my writing.
● I can write a glossary.
● I can write in the past tense because this is historical information.
● I can write in the third person.

Setting the context
Children will use bullet-point facts as the basis for writing an information text about dinosaurs. Children should sort the bullet points into two groups and decide upon a heading for the whole text and subheadings for each paragraph. They should highlight technical words and list glossary entries. Display the success criteria for children to refer to during the activity.

Assessment opportunity
Ask the children to complete the activity using the photocopiable page 'Non-fiction 2 Writing assessment'. Look for children's ability to organise their writing and to construct paragraphs. Is the style of writing clear and the purpose easily understood? Have they used vocabulary effectively?

Assessment evidence
This activity gathers evidence against Writing AF2, AF3, AF4 and AF7. Use the completed activity and children's work from the rest of this unit to make level judgements for Writing.

NON-FICTION

Name _____   Date _____

Information text spidergram

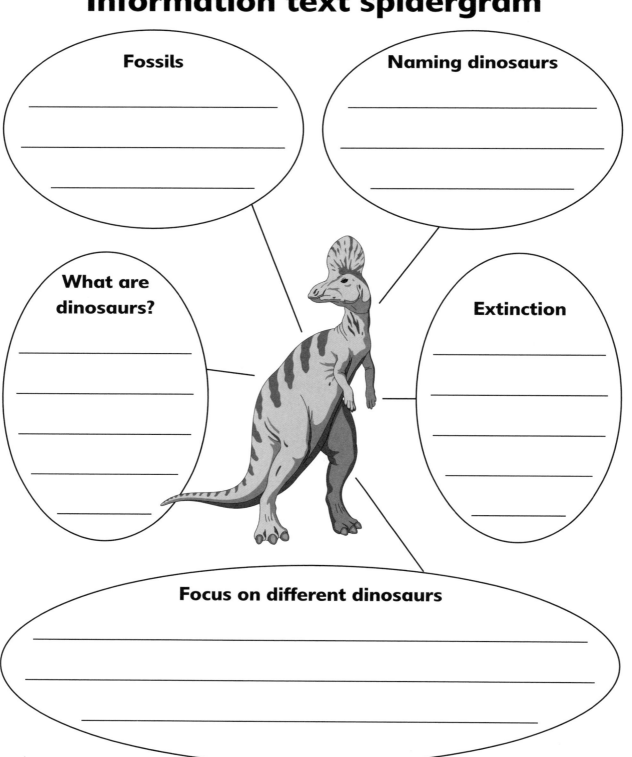

Fossils

_____
_____
_____

Naming dinosaurs

_____
_____
_____

What are dinosaurs?

_____
_____
_____
_____

Extinction

_____
_____
_____
_____

Focus on different dinosaurs

_____
_____
_____

Red
Amber
Green

I can use a spidergram to plan my research. ☐

I know where to look to find the information I need. ☐

Illustration © Nova Development

Name   Date

Research notes

Expert group number: _____

Area of research: _____

Question number 1:

Key words I will use to locate this information: _____

_____

Information I have found (in note form/bullet points): _____

_____

Details of diagrams/photographs/pictures to support written notes:

_____

Information source: _____

_____

Question number 2:

Key words I will use to locate this information: _____

_____

Information I have found (in note form/bullet points)_____

_____

Details of diagrams/photographs/pictures to support written notes:

_____

Information source: _____

_____

Red	◯	I can use an internet search engine to find information. ☐
Amber	◯	I can scan a non-fiction text to find information. ☐
Green	◯	I can make notes. ☐

Name   Date

Non-fiction 2 Reading assessment

1. List three features of the text that tell you it is an information text:

_____

2. Which words from the text would you find in a glossary at the back of the book? How do you know?

_____

3. Which section would tell you about the smallest dinosaur?

_____

4. How big is the smallest known dinosaur?

_____

5. How many different species have been found so far? (Clue: use your scanning skills to find a number.)

_____

6. How can we find out about dinosaurs?

_____

7. Name three different types of dinosaur:

_____

8. How are the types of dinosaur that are described listed?

_____

9. Why is this a useful way to display information?

_____

10. What was the name of the man who created the name 'dinosaur'?

_____

11. What evolved during the Jurassic period?

_____

Red
Amber
Green

I can use an information text to identify facts. ☐

I can find features of organisation in an information text. ☐

Non-fiction 2 Writing assessment

◼ Read all the bullet points.

◼ Sort them into two groups by highlighting using two colours.

◼ Number the bullet points in the order in which you will use them.

◼ Write the bullet points up in full sentences to create two paragraphs of information text.

◼ Underline words that you think would be included in a glossary – use a real glossary or dictionary to help you write your definitions!

◼ Choose a heading and subheadings for your work.

- Dinosaur means "terrible lizard".

- All dinosaurs had four limbs – some walked on back legs, some on all four.

- Dinosaurs lived on land (not in air or water).

- Most fossils are found in sedimentary rock.

- Some were meat eaters – carnivores.

- Fossils = remains or traces of ancient life.

- All fossils = one thing in common = at least 10,000 years old.

- Most were plant eaters – herbivores.

- Lived 65–245 million years ago.

- Fossils can be mineralized bones, teeth, shells, wood or actual unaltered material from an organism, such as frozen mammoth flesh, bones and fur.

- Three periods of time when dinosaurs lived. Different dinosaurs in different periods.

- Not all reptiles in those times were dinosaurs.

- Oldest known fossils are 3.5 billion years old.

- Largest was Barosaurus 80 feet (24 metres) tall.

- Eggs, nests, footprints leaf impressions, burrows and droppings are examples of trace fossils.

- Sedimentary rocks are made of sand, silt, mud or cobbles.

NON-FICTION
UNIT 3 Explanation texts

Literacy objectives

Speak and listen for a wide range of purposes in different contexts
Strand 1 Speaking
● Respond appropriately to the contributions of others in the light of differing viewpoints.

Read and write for a range of purposes on paper and on screen
Strand 7 Understanding and interpreting texts
● Use knowledge of different organisational features of texts to find information effectively.
Strand 8 Engaging with and responding to texts
● Read extensively favourite authors or genres and experiment with other types of texts.

● Interrogate texts to deepen and clarify understanding and response.
Strand 9 Creating and shaping texts
● Develop and refine ideas in writing using planning and problem-solving strategies.
● Summarise and shape material and ideas from different sources to write convincing and informative non-narrative texts.
Strand 10 Text structure and organisation
● Organise text into paragraphs to distinguish between different information, events or processes.
● Use adverbs and conjunctions to establish cohesion within paragraphs.
Strand 11 Sentence structure and punctuation
● Clarify meaning and point of view by using varied sentence structure (phrases, clauses and adverbials).

Key aspects of learning

Enquiry
● Children will ask questions arising from viewing a short film. They will investigate a range of texts, research and then plan how to present information effectively.
Creative thinking
● Children will generate and extend imaginative ideas to explain a process. They will suggest hypotheses, responding imaginatively through drama and talk, and respond to problems in order to create a written outcome.
Information processing
● Children will identify relevant information from a range of sources on paper and on screen and use this to write their own explanation texts.
Reasoning
● Children will use different sources to develop the language of cause and effect. They will draw inferences and conclusions to clarify, extend and follow up ideas in their oral and written work.
Evaluation
● Children will present information orally, diagrammatically and in writing. They will discuss success criteria, give feedback to others and judge effectiveness of their own work.

Assessment focuses

Reading
AF2 (*understand, describe, select or retrieve information, events or ideas from texts and use quotation and reference to text*).
AF4 (*identify and comment on the structure and organisation of texts, including grammatical and presentational features at text level*).

Writing
AF2 (*produce texts which are appropriate to task, reader and purpose*).
AF3 (*organise and present whole texts effectively, sequencing and structuring information, ideas and events*).
AF5 (*vary sentences for clarity, purpose and effect*).

Speaking and listening
Speaking (speak clearly with pace and use appropriate detail).

Resources

Phase 1 activities
Photocopiable page, 'Life cycle of a flowering plant'
Photocopiable page, 'Life cycle of a flowering plant: flow chart'
Interactive activity, 'Life cycle of a flowering plant'
Photocopiable page, 'Explanation text: checklist'
Interactive activity, 'Don't get tense about tenses!'
Photocopiable page, 'Text (a)'
Photocopiable page, 'Text (b)'
Photocopiable page, 'Text (c)'
Interactive activity, 'Report, recount or explanation?'
Phase 2 activities
Film clip, *The Soccamatic* (available on the BBC website at http://news.bbc.co.uk/2/hi/ entertainment/2314339.stm)
Photocopiable page, 'Diagram of the Soccamatic machine'
Interactive activity, 'Diagram of the Soccamatic machine'
Phase 3 activities
Photocopiable pages, 'Soccamatic machine manual' (versions 1 and 2)
Periodic assessment
Photocopiable page, 'Non-fiction 3 Reading assessment text'
Photocopiable page, 'Non-fiction 3 Reading assessment'
Photocopiable page, 'Non-fiction 3 Writing assessment'

Unit 3 ▢ Explanation texts

Learning outcomes	Assessment opportunity and evidence	Assessment focuses (AFs)		Success criteria
		Level 2	Level 3	
Phase ① activities pages 119-121				
Explanation texts and diagrams Children can use their knowledge of the organisational features of explanation texts to find information quickly.	● Independent activity where children retrieve information to create a flow chart. ● Children's completed flow charts.	**Reading AF2** ● Some specific, straightforward information recalled. ● Generally clear idea of where to look for information. **Writing AF3** ● Some basic sequencing of ideas or material. ● Opening and/or closings sometimes signalled.	**Reading AF2** ● Simple, most obvious points identified though there may also be some misunderstanding. ● Some comments include quotations from or references to text, but not always relevant. **Writing AF3** ● Some attempt to organise ideas with related points placed next to each other. ● Openings and closings usually signalled. ● Some attempt to sequence ideas or material logically.	● I can summarise information from an explanation text in a labelled flow chart. ● I can draw and label a flow chart that explains a process.
Features of an explanation text Children can use examples of explanation texts to identify key features: the purpose; structure; language features and presentational features.	● Independent activity where children identify the features of an explanation text. ● Children's annotated texts.	**Reading AF4** Some awareness of use of features of organisation.	**Reading AF4** A few basic features of organisation at text level identified, with little or no linked comment.	I can identify the key features of explanation texts and label them.
Report, recount or explanation? Children can use examples of explanation texts to identify key features: the purpose; structure; language features and presentational features.	● Independent activity where children complete an interactive activity to identify three text types. ● Completed interactive activity.	**Reading AF4** Some awareness of use of features of organisation.	**Reading AF4** A few basic features of organisation at text level identified, with little or no linked comment.	I can tell the difference between an explanation, a report and a recount.
Phase ② activities pages 122-123				
The Soccamatic machine (1) Children can orally explain a process or answer to a question using language features of the text type.	● Group discussion and role play where children explain how a machine works. ● Children's oral contributions.	**Reading AF4** Some awareness of use of features of organisation.	**Reading AF4** A few basic features of organisation at text level identified, with little or no linked comment.	● I can explain how something works using causal connectives to give reasons. ● I can talk about the structure and language features of an explanation text.
The Soccamatic machine (2) Children can create a flow diagram of a written explanation.	● Independent activity where children create a flow chart to explain how a machine works. ● Children's completed flow charts.	**Writing AF2** ● Some basic purpose established. ● Some appropriate features of the given form used. ● Some attempts to adopt appropriate style.	**Writing AF2** ● Purpose established at a general level. ● Main features of selected form sometimes signalled to the reader. ● Some attempts at appropriate style, with attention to reader.	I can plan an explanation using a labelled diagram.

Unit 3 📖 Explanation texts

Learning outcomes	Assessment opportunity and evidence	Assessment focuses (AFs)		Success criteria
		Level 2	**Level 3**	

Phase ③ activities page 124

Learning outcomes	Assessment opportunity and evidence	Level 2	Level 3	Success criteria
The Soccamatic machine – an explanation Children can write an explanation text from a diagrammatic plan using the conventions of the text type.	● Peer assessment where children evaluate explanation writing against the success criteria. ● Children's written explanations and feedback.	**Writing AF2** ● Some basic purpose established. ● Some appropriate features of the given form used. ● Some attempts to adopt appropriate style.	**Writing AF2** ● Purpose established at a general level. ● Main features of selected form sometimes signalled to the reader. ● Some attempts at appropriate style, with attention to reader.	● I can produce a written explanation using the key features of an explanation text. ● I can use time connectives to start each paragraph and causal connectives to link what happens.

Learning outcomes	Assessment opportunity and evidence	Assessment focuses (AFs)		Success criteria
		Level 4	**Level 5**	

Phase ① activities pages 119–121

Learning outcomes	Assessment opportunity and evidence	Level 4	Level 5	Success criteria
Explanation texts and diagrams Children can use their knowledge of the organisational features of explanation texts to find information quickly.	● Independent activity where children retrieve information to create a flow chart. ● Children's completed flow charts.	**Reading AF2** ● Some relevant points identified. ● Comments supported by some generally relevant textual reference or quotation. **Writing AF3** ● Ideas organised by clustering related points or by time sequence. ● Ideas are organised simply with a fitting opening and closing, sometimes linked. ● Ideas or material generally in logical sequence but overall direction of writing not always clearly signalled.	**Reading AF2** ● Most relevant points clearly identified, including those selected from different places in the text. ● Comments generally supported by relevant textual reference or quotation, even when points made are not always accurate. **Writing AF3** ● Material is structured clearly, with sentences organised into appropriate paragraphs. ● Development of material is effectively managed across text. ● Overall direction of the text supported by clear links between paragraphs.	● I can summarise information from an explanation text in a labelled flow chart. ● I can draw and label a flow chart that explains a process.
Features of an explanation text Children can use examples of explanation texts to identify key features: the purpose; structure; language features and presentational features.	● Independent activity where children identify the features of an explanation text. ● Children's annotated texts.	**Reading AF4** ● Some structural choices identified with simple comment. ● Some basic features of organisation at text level identified.	**Reading AF4** ● Comments on structural choices show some general awareness of writer's craft. ● Various features relating to organisation at text level, including form, are clearly identified.	I can identify the key features of explanation texts and label them.

Unit 3 ▪ Explanation texts

Learning outcomes	Assessment opportunity and evidence	Assessment focuses (AFs)		Success criteria
		Level 4	Level 5	
Report, recount or explanation? Children can use examples of explanation texts to identify key features: the purpose; structure; language features and presentational features.	● Independent activity where children complete an interactive activity to identify three text types. ● Completed interactive activity.	**Reading AF4** ● Some structural choices identified with simple comment. ● Some basic features of organisation at text level identified.	**Reading AF4** ● Comments on structural choices show some general awareness of writer's craft. ● Various features relating to organisation at text level, including form, are clearly identified.	I can tell the difference between an explanation, a report and a recount.

Phase ② activities pages 122-123

Learning outcomes	Assessment opportunity and evidence	Level 4	Level 5	Success criteria
The Soccamatic machine (1) Children can orally explain a process or answer to a question using language features of the text type.	● Group discussion and role play where children explain how a machine works. ● Children's oral contributions.	**Reading AF4** ● Some structural choices identified with simple comment. ● Some basic features of organisation at text level identified.	**Reading AF4** ● Comments on structural choices show some general awareness of writer's craft. ● Various features relating to organisation at text level, including form, are clearly identified.	● I can explain how something works using causal connectives to give reasons. ● I can talk about the structure and language features of an explanation text.
The Soccamatic machine (2) Children can create a flow diagram of a written explanation.	● Independent activity where children create a flow chart to explain how a machine works. ● Children's completed flow charts.	**Writing AF2** ● Main purpose of writing is clear but not always consistently maintained. ● Main features of selected form are clear and appropriate to purpose. ● Style generally appropriate to task, though awareness of reader not always sustained.	**Writing AF2** ● Main purpose of writing is clear and consistently maintained. ● Features of selected form clearly established with some adaptation to purpose. ● Appropriate style clearly established to maintain reader's interest throughout.	I can plan an explanation using a labelled diagram.

Phase ③ activities page 124

Learning outcomes	Assessment opportunity and evidence	Level 4	Level 5	Success criteria
The Soccamatic machine - an explanation Children can write an explanation text from a diagrammatic plan using the conventions of the text type.	● Peer assessment where children evaluate explanation writing against the success criteria. ● Children's written explanations and feedback.	**Writing AF2** ● Main purpose of writing is clear but not always consistently maintained. ● Main features of selected form are clear and appropriate to purpose. ● Style generally appropriate to task, though awareness of reader not always sustained.	**Writing AF2** ● Main purpose of writing is clear and consistently maintained. ● Features of selected form clearly established with some adaptation to purpose. ● Appropriate style clearly established to maintain reader's interest throughout.	● I can produce a written explanation using the key features of an explanation text. ● I can use time connectives to start each paragraph and causal connectives to link what happens.

Phase ① Explanation texts and diagrams

Learning outcome
Children can use their knowledge of the organisational features of explanation texts to find information quickly.

Success criteria
- I can summarise information from an explanation text in a labelled flow chart.
- I can draw and label a flow chart that explains a process.

Setting the context
Tell the children that 'to explain' is to give an answer to a question or to describe how a process, for example in nature, works. Often language is insufficient to complete the explanation and it can be easier to support a verbal explanation with a diagram (such as a plan, map or flow chart) that can be pointed to in order to show movement and direction. Tell the children that they are going to read an explanatory text about the life cycle of a flowering plant and use the written information to create an annotated flow chart to complement the written information.

Assessment opportunity
Give all the children the photocopiable pages 'Life cycle of a flowering plant' and 'Life cycle of a flowering plant: flow chart'. Tell them to read the text extract carefully and to highlight the words and phrases that they think are most important. Tell them that this is the information they are going to put into their flow chart. As the children are reading and highlighting, ask questions to help them to focus and you to assess their learning, such as: *Which information is not necessary in a flow chart? What information is essential and will help to explain the process for the reader?* When they have finished highlighting the text, ask them to construct their flow chart, using the highlighted text. Assess how well children are able to identify information from a text and use it to produce a text which demonstrates an ability to organise information into a logical sequence.

Assessment evidence
The completed flow charts and annotated text extracts will indicate whether children are able to read and understand an explanation text and extract information from it. It will also show whether children are able to organise and present ideas in a logical sequence. This activity will produce evidence against Reading AF2 and Writing AF3.

Next steps
Support: Children can use the interactive activity 'Life cycle of a flowering plant' to click and drag statements into the appropriate stages of the life cycle before attempting to create a written version. Support their understanding by discussing the meanings of scientific vocabulary.
Extension: During ICT sessions, children can practise annotating diagrams in response to a text, for example, by using the BBC Schools Bitesize revision activities for Science and Geography.

Key aspects of learning
Information processing: Children will identify relevant information from a range of sources on paper and on screen and use this to write their own explanation texts.
Reasoning: Children will use different sources to develop the language of cause and effect. They will draw inferences and conclusions to clarify, extend and follow up ideas in their oral and written work.
Evaluation: Children will present information orally, diagrammatically and in writing. They will discuss success criteria, give feedback to others and judge effectiveness of their own work.

Phase ① Features of an explanation text

Learning outcome
Children can use examples of explanation texts to identify key features: the purpose; structure; language features and presentational features.

Success criteria
I can identify the key features of explanation texts and label them.

Setting the context
Ask the children to find a talk partner and ask the pairs to work together to list what they think are the key features of an explanation text. Listen to their discussions. Bring the whole class back together and establish an agreed definition. Recap the features of an explanation text with the children: they explain how and why something happens (rather than just recounting what happens). They are often organised into logical stages, and are written in the present tense. They often have features such as headings, subheadings and diagrams.

Assessment opportunity
Give children photocopiable page 'Explanation text: checklist' and a photocopy of an explanation text that you have selected. Ask them to use the checklist to annotate the features of the explanation text. Some of the features will be more evident than others. Some children may need guidance when identifying language features. Lead children to identify the verb in each sentence and ask: *Which tense is it in?* Encourage the children to identify the connectives that link the explanation of the process together. Assess how well children are able to identify the relevant organisational and language features of a text type.

Assessment evidence
At levels 2–3, children will be able to identify features such as headings, subheadings and bullet points. At levels 4–5, children will be able to identify grammatical as well as presentational features and will be able to explain the purpose of some of these. The annotated texts will provide evidence against Reading AF4.

Next steps
Support: Have children use the interactive activity 'Don't get tense about tenses!' to help them identify verbs in the past and present tense.
Extension: During a library session, challenge children to find a selection of explanatory texts that answer a specific question, for example, *Can you find texts that explain how sedimentary rocks are formed?* Invite them to present their findings, giving their own explanation as to why one explanatory text is better than another.

Key aspects of learning
Enquiry: Children will investigate a range of texts, research and then plan how to present information effectively.
Reasoning: Children will use different sources to develop the language of cause and effect. They will draw inferences and conclusions to clarify, extend and follow up ideas in their oral and written work.
Evaluation: Children will present information orally, diagrammatically and in writing.

Phase ① Report, recount or explanation?

Learning outcome
Children can use examples of explanation texts to identify key features: the purpose; structure; language features and presentational features.

Success criteria
I can tell the difference between an explanation, a report and a recount.

Setting the context
This activity will enable children to consolidate their understanding of the distinction between three closely related text types: recounts, reports and explanations. With the whole class, look at sample texts and the NLS Non-Fiction Flyers, 5 (recount), 7 (report) and 8 (explanation) to make comparisons between the three genres. Establish the similarities, for example, all three text types provide information. Then discuss the differences: recounts and historical reports are written in the past tense whereas explanations are generally written in the present tense. (Note: non-historical reports are written in the present tense.) Recounts retell events in chronological order; reports describe what something is or was like and tend not to be chronologically ordered; and explanations explain how or why something works and are usually organised sequentially.

Assessment opportunity
Following the introduction, the children can use independently the interactive activity 'Report, recount or explanation?' to identify the text types on the photocopiable pages 'Text (a)', 'Text (b)' and 'Text (c)'. Ask them to read the three text extracts and then use the radio buttons in the interactive activity to define which features each text displays. In this way they will demonstrate their knowledge of verb tenses and connectives. They will also have to search for pronouns to establish whether the text makes reference to participants. This activity establishes whether children are able to identify language features of non-fiction texts.

Assessment evidence
At levels 2–3 children will demonstrate awareness of basic language features of non-fiction texts. At levels 4–5, children will identify and comment on grammatical features of the texts. This activity provides evidence against mainly Reading AF4 (see also Reading AF7).

Next steps
Support: Print off the three texts and give a copy to each child. Read and discuss the texts in a group before attempting the interactive activity.
Extension: Ask children to source further examples of each text type and validate their choice by explaining which features are present.

Key aspects of learning
Information processing: Children will identify relevant information from a range of sources on paper and on screen and use this to write their own explanation texts.
Reasoning: Children will use different sources to develop the language of cause and effect. They will draw inferences and conclusions to clarify, extend and follow up ideas in their oral and written work.

Unit 3 ☐ **Explanation texts**

Phase ② The Soccamatic machine (1)

Learning outcome
Children can orally explain a process or answer to a question using language features of the text type.

Success criteria
- I can explain how something works using causal connectives to give reasons.
- I can talk about the structure and language features of an explanation text.

Setting the context
The children need to have explored the language features of explanatory texts, especially use of simple present tense and construction of cause-and-effect type statements including the use of causal connectives. Find out if the children are familiar with the Wallace & Gromit films. Explain that Aardman Animations Ltd produced a series of one-minute movies featuring Wallace and his pet dog Gromit, entitled 'Cracking Contraptions'. Each movie features a different invention that Wallace has built or purchased to help him around the home – the Autochef, the Bully Proof Vest, for example. Watch the movie, *The Soccamatic* (free to view on the BBC's website at http://news.bbc.co.uk/2/hi/entertainment/2314339.stm).

Assessment opportunity
After watching the film, explain that unfortunately, Wallace hasn't written a manual to accompany the machine and so is having difficulty selling it. Divide the children into groups of five and ask them to role play the process and then discuss how the Soccamatic machine works, for example, pushing it into position, starting the machine so the football boots rotate, lifting the lever to load the footballs and so on. Encourage the children to act out different roles such as being the moving parts of the machine, the machine operator or the goalkeeper. Provide opportunities to re-watch the movie to ensure children can identify and link the different stages of operation. Circulate round the groups listening to their discussions. Ask prompt questions such as: *What is the purpose of the Soccamatic machine? How does it work? Where does the operator position the machine? Why? What happens when the lever is raised?* Listen for the children's use of causal connectives and time connectives (for example, 'so', 'next') and simple present tense in their explanations. Then, ask the children how they would go about writing an explanatory text for the Soccamatic manual. *What would you use for a title? What would you include in an introductory paragraph? How will you make your explanations clear for your reader?* Their opinions on how they would write the manual will reflect their understanding of the organisational features of explanation texts.

Assessment evidence
At levels 2–3, children will mention a few organisational features of explanation texts when describing how to write the manual. At levels 4–5, children will comment on organisational features. Use this activity provide evidence against Reading AF4.

Next steps
Support: Have children re-watch the video in short clips. After each, discuss what they have seen and model how this could be reflected in a written explanation.
Extension: Encourage children to report back the group's ideas to the class.

Key aspects of learning
Enquiry: Children will ask questions arising from viewing a short film. They will investigate a range of texts, research and then plan how to present information effectively.
Creative thinking: Children will generate and extend imaginative ideas to explain a process. They will suggest hypotheses, responding imaginatively through drama and talk, and respond to problems in order to create a written outcome.
Reasoning: Children will use different sources to develop the language of cause and effect. They will draw inferences and conclusions to clarify, extend and follow up ideas in their oral and written work.

Phase ② The Soccamatic machine (2)

Learning outcome
Children can create a flow diagram of a written explanation.

Success criteria
I can plan an explanation using a labelled diagram.

Setting the context
This activity assumes that children have carried out the previous activity. Having watched the movie several times and discussed the operation of the machine, explain to the children that they are going to create an annotated diagram of how the Soccamatic machine works. Recall the order of operation as a class.

Assessment opportunity
Give the children the photocopiable page 'Diagram of the Soccamatic machine' and ask them to number the boxes on the photograph and then write a description of how each stage of the process works. For example, '1. The operator wheels the machine onto the pitch and positions it in front of the goal.' Children will demonstrate their ability to clearly record and explain the processes involved and adopt an appropriate style of writing. Can they sequence the stages in the process of using it? Can they use the appropriate language features such as simple present tense, or passive voice? Can they explain cause and effect? For example, '3. When the operator pushes the lever down this causes the football boots to spin.' Can they use causal connectives? For example, '6. The operator raises the lever so that the barrel reloads...' Assess how well the children are able to write purposefully and in an appropriate style. Gather in the completed sheets at the end of the activity.

Assessment evidence
At levels 2–3, children will establish purpose in their writing at a basic or a general level and they may attempt to adopt an appropriate style of writing. At levels 4–5, the main purpose of the children's writing will be clear and their style of writing will be appropriate to the task. The activity will provide evidence against Writing AF2 (see also Writing AF5).

Next steps
Support: Have less confident learners use the interactive activity 'Diagram of the Soccamatic machine' to drag and drop explanatory captions into the appropriate locations on the photograph to create an annotated diagram.
Extension: Ask children to create a flow chart to accompany the annotated diagram.

Key aspects of learning
Creative thinking: Children will generate and extend imaginative ideas to explain a process. They will suggest hypotheses, responding imaginatively through drama and talk, and respond to problems in order to create a written outcome.
Reasoning: Children will use different sources to develop the language of cause and effect. They will draw inferences and conclusions to clarify, extend and follow up ideas in their oral and written work.
Evaluation: Children will present information orally, diagrammatically and in writing.

Unit 3 **Explanation texts**

Phase ③ The Soccamatic machine - an explanation

Success criteria
● I can produce a written explanation using the key features of an explanation text.
● I can use time connectives to start each paragraph and causal connectives to link what happens.

Setting the context
Having created an annotated diagram of the operation of the Soccamatic machine in the previous activity, tell the children that they are going to write an explanation of the process for a page in the Soccamatic machine manual. Recap on the key features of the explanatory texts using the photocopiable page 'Explanation text: checklist' and the success criteria. Emphasise the need to use time and causal connectives, and simple present tense. Provide access to the checklist of features to assist their writing. Give them the photocopiable page 'Soccamatic machine manual' (versions 1 or 2) to use as a writing frame.

Assessment opportunity
Encourage the children to swap manuals and assess their peer's work against the success criteria and features checklist. Have they incorporated the features of explanation texts? Have they included headings and subheadings? Is there an introductory paragraph or sentence explaining the function of the machine? Does each stage logically follow on from the next? Have they used causal and time connectives to encourage the flow of their writing? Have they written in the third person and the simple present tense? Gather in the completed manuals at the end of the activity. Assess whether the children are able to maintain the style of the text type, their ability to adhere to the purpose of the writing and whether they have adopted a style which will maintain the reader's interest throughout.

Assessment evidence
At levels 2–3, children will establish purpose in their writing at a basic or a general level and they may attempt to adopt an appropriate style of writing. At levels 4–5, the main purpose of the children's writing will be clear and their style of writing will be appropriate to the task of writing an explanatory manual. Use this activity to gather evidence against Writing AF2.

Next steps
Support: Provide children with prepared phrases on card so they can practise constructing cause-and-effect statements and using causal connectives.
Extension: More confident learners may invent their own Wallace and Gromit-style machine and construct it as part of a D&T project. They can follow this up by writing their own machine manual, adopting the features of the text genre.

Key aspects of learning
Creative thinking: Children will generate and extend imaginative ideas to explain a process. They will suggest hypotheses, responding imaginatively through drama and talk, and respond to problems in order to create a written outcome.
Information processing: Children will identify relevant information from a range of sources on paper and on screen and use this to write their own explanation texts.
Reasoning: Children will use different sources to develop the language of cause and effect. They will draw inferences and conclusions to clarify, extend and follow up ideas in their oral and written work.
Evaluation: Children will present information orally, diagrammatically and in writing. They will discuss success criteria, give feedback to others and judge effectiveness of their own work.

Periodic assessment

Reading

Learning outcome	
Children can create a flow diagram of a written explanation.	**Success criteria** I can use an explanation text to create a flow chart that supports the text. **Setting the context** This activity links to learning about materials in science. Ask the children to imagine that they are writing a science textbook for Year 4 children. Explain that the text has been written but the author has given them the job of creating a flow chart to accompany and support the text. **Assessment opportunity** Give the children the photocopiable page 'Non-fiction 3 Reading assessment text' to read the extract about solids, liquids and gases. They will then use the photocopiable page 'Non-fiction 3 Reading assessment' to create a flow diagram which explains the process of change from a solid, to a liquid and then to a gas. Assess whether children can identify key points from a text. Can they establish meaning and use this to assist them in their writing? **Assessment evidence** This activity gathers evidence towards mainly Reading AF2 but also AF4. Use this activity as well as samples of children's reading throughout the unit to assess their overall level in Reading.

Writing

Learning outcome	
Children can write an explanation text from a diagrammatic plan using the conventions of the text type.	**Success criteria** ● I can use a flow chart to write an explanation. ● I can use headings and subheadings. ● I can include an introductory sentence or paragraph. ● I can use the simple present tense. ● I can use time and causal connectives. ● I can use technical words. ● I can create a glossary at the end to explain technical words. **Setting the context** This activity links to learning in science. Children can use the information from a food chain flow chart to write an explanation text independently. Display the success criteria for the children to refer to during the activity. **Assessment opportunity** Ask the children to write an explanation based on the flow chart from the photocopiable page 'Non-fiction 3 Writing assessment'. Encourage them to refer to the success criteria to refine and improve their writing. Assess their ability to write using the features of explanation texts. Can they utilise the flow chart provided? Do they draw on their own knowledge when writing? **Assessment evidence** Children will demonstrate a varying awareness and understanding of the organisational and language features of the text type. Gather evidence against Writing AF2 and AF3. Use this activity to make a level judgement about their overall progress in Writing.

Explanation text: checklist

■ You will know if a text is an explanation text if you can spot some of these features (not all of them will be in every text!)

1. Third person title (which may contain the words "how" or "why")

2. An introductory paragraph which introduces the subject to the reader

3. Bullet points or numbered steps written in a logical order

4. Subheadings

5. Labelled diagrams or plans or maps or charts which help to explain the text

6. Flow charts to show how a process works

7. Causal connectives (eg "if", "this results in", "because", "so that")

8. Time connectives (eg "whenever", "after", "finally")

9. A glossary of technical terms used in the text

10. Simple present tense.

Non-fiction 3 Reading assessment text

Solids, liquids and gases

Solids

A solid stays in one place and does not flow and does not spread out like a gas. It keeps its shape and can be held in your hand (if it's not too heavy).

A solid can be shaped, for example, modelling clay. Don't get confused! Salt and sand are both solids even though they can be poured. This is because each particle of sand or salt stays the same shape. If a solid is heated it can turn into a liquid, for example: an ice cream is a solid which will melt in the sunshine. (It's best to eat it quickly!)

Liquids

A liquid will take on the shape of the container it is in. It does flow and it can be poured. It is not easy to hold a liquid in your hand – think about what happens when you cup your hands to collect water to wash your face! Even though it changes shape, it keeps the same volume.

If we heat a liquid it can turn into a gas. When water is boiled it becomes steam.

If we cool a liquid it can become a solid. When water is cooled it becomes ice (at 0°C).

Gases

Gases do not keep their shape; they spread out to fill the space they are in. Their volume does not stay the same either. Think about what happens when you let go of a balloon full of air – the gas (air) escapes and spreads out into the atmosphere.

Gases can be squashed – this is what happens when we pump up our bicycle tyres – we are squashing air into a fixed container.

If we cool some gases they can become liquid (steam will become water if it is cooled).

Heat

Heat can change a solid into a liquid and a liquid into a gas.

If a solid is heated to become a liquid we say it has melted.

If a liquid is heated and becomes a gas we say it has evaporated.

If a gas is cooled to become a liquid we say it has condensed.

If a liquid is cooled to become a solid we say it has frozen.

NON-FICTION

Name   Date

Non-fiction 3 Reading assessment

■ Create a flow chart that shows the characteristics of solids, liquids and gases and how they change between states.

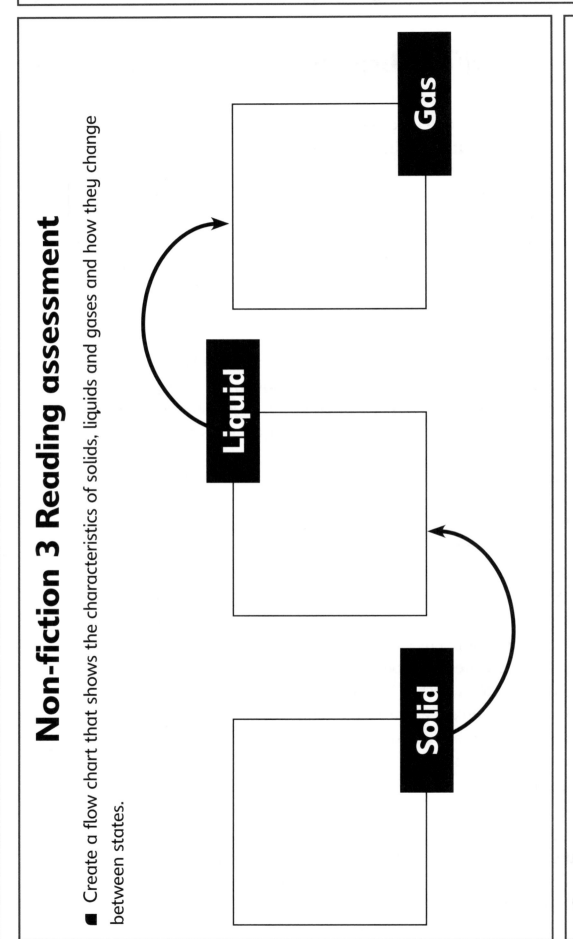

I can use an explanation text to create a flow chart that supports the text. ☐

Red
Amber
Green

Non-fiction 3 Writing assessment

■ Use the information from the flow chart below to write a text that explains food chains.

A cat is a carnivore. It eats other small animals so it is called a predator. The animals it eats are called its prey.

This is why we must help to protect our environment and all the creatures and plants in it.

A sparrow is an omnivore. It eats plants and small insects to get its energy.

If a disease wipes out a species such as a certain type of caterpillar, then it affects the whole food chain.

A caterpillar is a herbivore. It gets energy by eating leaves.

Animals get energy by eating other plants and animals. They are called consumers.

Green plants are called producers because they make their own energy by photosynthesis. They usually start the food chain.

Plants make their own energy by photosynthesis. They are called producers. They are at the start of the food chain.

All living things need food to survive – to give them energy.

Illustration © Bill Houston / Bill Houston Creative Limited.

NON-FICTION
UNIT 4 Persuasive texts

Literacy objectives

Speak and listen for a wide range of purposes in different contexts
Strand 1 Speaking
- Respond appropriately to the contributions of others in the light of differing viewpoints.

Strand 2 Listening and responding
- Compare the different contributions of music, words and images in short extracts from TV programmes.
- Identify how talk varies with age, familiarity, gender and purpose.

Read and write for a range of purposes on paper and on screen
Strand 7 Understanding and interpreting texts
- Explain how writers use figurative and expressive language to create images and atmosphere.

Strand 8 Engaging with and responding to texts
- Interrogate texts to deepen and clarify understanding and response.

Strand 9 Creating and shaping texts
- Develop and refine ideas in writing using planning and problem-solving strategies.
- Summarise and shape material and ideas from different sources to write convincing and informative non-narrative texts.
- Show imagination through the language used to create emphasis, humour, atmosphere or suspense.
- Choose and combine words, images and other features for particular effects.

Strand 11 Sentence structure and punctuation
- Clarify meaning and point of view by using varied sentence structure (phrases, clauses and adverbials).

Strand 12 Presentation
- Use word-processing packages to present written work and continue to increase speed and accuracy in typing.

Key aspects of learning

Information processing
- Children locate and refer to relevant examples from a DVD text.

Reasoning
- Children will be able to give reasons for their opinions about the impact of a range of persuasive texts.

Evaluation
- Children will develop their own assessment criteria to evaluate persuasive texts. They will use these when reviewing their own work and the work of others.

Communication
- Children will develop their ability to discuss as they work collaboratively in pairs, groups and whole-class contexts. They will communicate persuasively orally, in writing and through ICT if appropriate.

Assessment focuses

Reading
AF2 (*understand, describe, select or retrieve information, events or ideas from texts and use quotation and reference to text*).
AF4 (*identify and comment on the structure and organisation of texts, including grammatical and presentational features at text level*).
AF6 (*identify and comment on writers' purposes and viewpoints, and the overall effect of the text on the reader*).

Writing
AF2 (*produce texts which are appropriate to task, reader and purpose*).
AF7 (*select appropriate and effective vocabulary*).

Speaking and listening
Speaking (speak with clarity, intonation and pace).
Listening and responding (respond appropriately).

Resources

Phase 1 activities
Photocopiable page, 'Advertisement (a)'
Photocopiable page, 'Advertisement (b)'
Photocopiable pages, 'Advertisement analysis' (versions 1 and 2)
Photocopiable page, 'Persuasive texts checklist'
Photocopiable pages, 'Film trailer evaluation' (versions 1 and 2)
Phase 2 activities
Photocopiable page, 'Rhetorical questions'
Interactive activity, 'Rhetorical questions'
Photocopiable page, 'Film trailer planning sheet'
Phase 3 activities
Photocopiable page, 'Voice-over script'
Periodic assessment
RSPB Youth website homepage, internet (www.rspb.org.uk/youth/)
Photocopiable page, 'Non-fiction 4 Reading assessment text'
Photocopiable page, 'Non-fiction 4 Reading assessment'

Unit 4 ◻ Persuasive texts

Learning outcomes	Assessment opportunity and evidence	Assessment focuses (AFs)		Success criteria
		Level 2	Level 3	
Phase ① activities pages 135–137				
What do you think? Children can express personal opinions to compare and contrast a range of texts using evidence from the text to support their opinion.	• Paired activity where children discuss the impact of adverts. • Children's oral contributions and completed photocopiable pages.	**Reading AF6** • Some awareness that writers have viewpoints and purposes. • Simple statements about likes and dislikes in reading, sometimes with reasons.	**Reading AF6** • Comments identify main purpose. • Express personal response but with little awareness of writer's viewpoint or effect on reader.	• I can say how adverts make me feel and give reasons. • I can find words in the text which explain my response.
Spot the persuasive feature Children can identify key language features in paper-based persuasive texts.	• Group activity where children analyse the key features of persuasive adverts. • Children's annotated adverts.	**Reading AF4** Some awareness of use of features of organisation.	**Reading AF4** A few basic features of organisation at text level identified, with little or no linked comment.	I can identify the key features of a persuasive text.
Film trailer evaluation Children can identify key language features in film-based persuasive texts.	• Group activity where children watch and then evaluate a film trailer. • Children's completed film trailer evaluation sheets.	**Reading AF2** • Some specific, straightforward information recalled. • Generally clear idea of where to look for information. **Writing AF7** • Simple, often speech-like vocabulary conveys relevant meanings. • Some adventurous word choices.	**Reading AF2** • Simple, most obvious points identified though there may also be some misunderstanding. • Some comments include quotations from or references to text, but not always relevant. **Writing AF7** • Simple, generally appropriate vocabulary used, limited in range. • Some words selected for effect or occasion.	• I can evaluate a film advert against the persuasive text features used. • I can identify the intended impact on an audience. • I can identify the intended impact of the images. • I can identify the intended impact of the music. • I can identify the intended impact of the voice-over words.
Phase ② activities pages 137–139				
Rhetorical questions Children can use key language features to plan a persuasive text.	• Independent activity where children write their own rhetorical questions. • Children's completed rhetorical sentences.	**Writing AF7** • Simple, often speech-like vocabulary conveys relevant meanings. • Some adventurous word choices.	**Writing AF7** • Simple, generally appropriate vocabulary used, limited in range. • Some words selected for effect or occasion.	• I can identify the meaning of a rhetorical question. • I can write rhetorical questions.
Planning a movie trailer Children can use key language features to plan a persuasive text.	• Group activity where children plan a film trailer. • Children's oral contributions and completed photocopiable pages.	**Writing AF7** • Simple, often speech-like vocabulary conveys relevant meanings. • Some adventurous word choices.	**Writing AF7** • Simple, generally appropriate vocabulary used, limited in range. • Some words selected for effect or occasion.	• I can select four clips from a movie to create a film trailer. • I can say what impact I want the soundtrack to have. • I can say what impact I want the voice-over script to have. • I can say what impact I want the images to have. • I can order the clips to build tension or interest.

Unit 4 ◻ Persuasive texts

Learning outcomes	Assessment opportunity and evidence	Assessment focuses (AFs)		Success criteria
		Level 2	Level 3	
Phase ③ activities page 139				
Writing the movie trailer Children can write a persuasive text using informal language and a range of simple connectives.	• Group activity where children write a voice-over script for a film clip. • Children's completed voice-over script.	**Writing AF2** • Some basic purpose established. • Some appropriate features of the given form used. • Some attempts to adopt appropriate style.	**Writing AF2** • Purpose established at a general level. • Main features of selected form sometimes signalled to the reader. • Some attempts at appropriate style, with attention to reader.	• I can write a script for my movie trailer voice-over. • I can add sound effects. • I can explain the kind of music I need to add to build tension or interest.

Learning outcomes	Assessment opportunity and evidence	Assessment focuses (AFs)		Success criteria
		Level 4	Level 5	
Phase ① activities pages 135–137				
What do you think? Children can express personal opinions to compare and contrast a range of texts using evidence from the text to support their opinion.	• Paired activity where children discuss the impact of adverts. • Children's oral contributions and completed photocopiable pages.	**Reading AF6** • Main purpose identified. • Simple comments show some awareness of writer's viewpoint. • Simple comment on overall effect on reader.	**Reading AF6** • Main purpose clearly identified, often through general overview. • Viewpoint in texts clearly identified, with some, often limited, explanation. • General awareness of effect on the reader, with some, often limited, explanation.	• I can say how adverts make me feel and give reasons. • I can find words in the text which explain my response.
Spot the persuasive feature Children can identify key language features in paper-based persuasive texts	• Group activity where children analyse the key features of persuasive adverts. • Children's annotated adverts.	**Reading AF4** • Some structural choices identified with simple comment. • Some basic features of organisation at text level identified.	**Reading AF4** • Comments on structural choices show general awareness of writer's craft. • Various features relating to organisation at text level, including form, are clearly identified.	I can identify the key features of a persuasive text.
Film trailer evaluation Children can identify key language features in film-based persuasive texts.	• Group activity where children watch and then evaluate a film trailer. • Children's completed film trailer evaluation sheets.	**Writing AF7** • Some evidence of deliberate vocabulary choices. • Some expansion of general vocabulary to match topic.	**Writing AF7** • Vocabulary chosen for effect. • Reasonably wide vocabulary used, though not always appropriately.	• I can evaluate a film advert against the persuasive text features used. • I can identify the intended impact on an audience. • I can identify the intended impact of the images. • I can identify the intended impact of the music. • I can identify the intended impact of the voice-over words.

Unit 4 Persuasive texts

Learning outcomes	Assessment opportunity and evidence	Assessment focuses (AFs)		Success criteria
		Level 4	Level 5	
Phase ② activities pages 137–139				
Rhetorical questions Children can use key language features to plan a persuasive text.	● Independent activity where children write their own rhetorical questions. ● Children's completed rhetorical sentences.	**Writing AF7** ● Some evidence of deliberate vocabulary choices. ● Some expansion of general vocabulary to match topic.	**Writing AF7** ● Vocabulary chosen for effect. ● Reasonably wide vocabulary used, though not always appropriately.	● I can identify the meaning of a rhetorical question. ● I can write rhetorical questions.
Planning a movie trailer Children can use key language features to plan a persuasive text.	● Group activity where children plan a film trailer. ● Children's oral contributions and completed photocopiable pages.	**Writing AF7** ● Some evidence of deliberate vocabulary choices ● Some expansion of general vocabulary to match topic.	**Writing AF7** ● Vocabulary chosen for effect. ● Reasonably wide vocabulary used, though not always appropriately.	● I can select four clips from a movie to create a film trailer. ● I can say what impact I want the soundtrack to have. ● I can say what impact I want the voice-over script to have. ● I can say what impact I want the images to have. ● I can order the clips to build tension or interest.
Phase ③ activities pages 139				
Writing the movie trailer Children can write a persuasive text using informal language and a range of simple connectives.	● Group activity where children write a voice-over script for a film clip. ● Children's completed voice-over script.	**Writing AF2** ● Main purpose of writing is clear but not always consistently maintained. ● Main features of selected form are clear and appropriate to purpose. ● Style generally appropriate to task, though awareness of reader not always sustained.	**Writing AF2** ● Main purpose of writing is clear and consistently maintained. ● Features of selected form clearly established with some adaptation to purpose. ● Appropriate style clearly established to maintain reader's interest throughout.	● I can write a script for my movie trailer voice-over. ● I can add sound effects. ● I can explain the kind of music I need to add to build tension or interest.

134 100 LITERACY ASSESSMENT LESSONS · YEAR 4   ■SCHOLASTIC

Phase ① What do you think?

Learning outcome
Children can express personal opinions to compare and contrast a range of texts using evidence from the text to support their opinion.

Success criteria
● I can say how adverts make me feel and give reasons.
● I can find words in the text which explain my response.

Setting the context
Present the children with three very different advertisements, two from the photocopiable pages 'Advertisement (a)' and 'Advertisement (b)' and one advert of your own choosing and tell them that they all have the same aim – to persuade the reader to act. Display the success criteria so the children can refer to them during the activity.

Assessment opportunity
Tell the children to work in pairs to read the adverts, to decide what they are trying to persuade the reader to do and how they are trying to make the reader feel and then to identify which words and phrases have been used to do this. Ask the children to write notes or annotate the sheets. Finally, ask them to look at other features of the adverts that are designed to create an impact, and describe what elements have been used and why. Come back together and discuss the findings as a class. This activity provides an initial assessment of how well the children can approach a new text type. Children working at levels 2–3 can record their notes on version 1 of the photocopiable page 'Advertisement analysis' and those working at levels 4–5 can use version 2 of the photocopiable page. Assess how well the children can identify the writer's purpose and how they achieve this. Are they also able to describe the effect that each advert has on them as readers?

Assessment evidence
At levels 2–3, children will identify the purpose of the adverts but they will have little awareness of the overall effect of the text on them as readers. At levels 4–5, children will identify the main purpose of each advert and will make comments on the effect on the audience. The activity will provide evidence against Reading AF6.

Next steps
Support: If children have difficulty in locating information in the text to back up their findings, provide a text and point out words and features. Ask questions to prompt children to explain why specific words were chosen.
Extension: Invite children to search through magazines and newspapers for advertisements that evoke a range of reactions. For example, can they find advertisements that make the reader feel pity, hunger, the desire to buy a product or watch a product? Can they verbally explain how the advertisements have created that impact?

Key aspects of learning
Reasoning: Children will be able to give reasons for their opinions about the impact of a range of persuasive texts.
Communication: Children will develop their ability to discuss as they work collaboratively in pairs, groups and whole-class contexts. They will communicate persuasively orally, in writing and through ICT if appropriate.

NON-FICTION

Phase ① Spot the persuasive feature

Learning outcome
Children can identify key language features in paper-based persuasive texts.

Success criteria
I can identify the key features of a persuasive text.

Setting the context
Split the class into ability groups. Give out copies of the two advertisements from the photocopiable pages 'Advertisement (a)' and 'Advertisement (b)' plus one advert of your own choosing (one for each child in the group) and a copy of the photocopiable page 'Persuasive texts checklist'.

Assessment opportunity
Each group can work together to identify and to highlight persuasive features in the advertisements and to annotate them using the checklist. Ask them to share their findings with another group and to add any features they have missed using a different coloured highlighter pen. Circulate around the groups and ask the children for feedback: *Did anyone find examples of strong punctuation? Did you highlight adjectives that are used to stir up emotions? Which adjectives did you identify? What impact do you think these were intended to have? Did you find an example of the conditional tense? What was it used for?*

Assessment evidence
At levels 2–3, children will identify some language and presentational features of the texts, such as powerful punctuation or use of colour. At levels 4–5, children will identify and comment on the structural and organisational features in the texts. Children's discussions and annotations will produce evidence against Reading AF4.

Next steps
Support: As a starting point for children who need to work on one feature at a time, locate all the adjectives in the text. Can they tell you why each adjective was used?
Extension: Challenge children to source advertisements that provide strong exemplification of each feature on the list. These examples can be used for display.

Key aspects of learning
Reasoning: Children will be able to give reasons for their opinions about the impact of a range of persuasive texts.
Evaluation: Children will develop their own assessment criteria to evaluate persuasive texts. They will use these when reviewing their own work and the work of others.
Communication: Children will develop their ability to discuss as they work collaboratively in pairs, groups and whole-class contexts. They will communicate persuasively orally, in writing and through ICT if appropriate.

Phase ① Film trailer evaluation

Learning outcome
Children can identify key language features in film-based persuasive texts.

Success criteria
● I can evaluate a film advert against persuasive text features used.
● I can identify the intended impact on an audience.
● I can identify the intended impact of the images.
● I can identify the intended impact of the music.
● I can identify the intended impact of the voice-over words.

Setting the context
Children will need to have had experience of assessing the features of written persuasive texts. Give the children a film trailer, from a popular children's movie, to watch (ensure your choice of trailer is suitably rated). *Madagascar: Escape 2 Africa*

(www.madagascar-themovie.com) is a fun choice that provides good examples of the different features. The activity can be done using trailers at the start of a DVD or online. Explain that the producers created the trailer with the intention of encouraging the public to want to see the film. The task is to unpick the intentions of the trailer producers. What impact did they want to have on the viewer? Display the success criteria so children can refer to them during the activity.

Assessment opportunity
Give the children working at levels 2–3 version 1 of the photocopiable page 'Film trailer evaluation'. Children working at levels 4–5 can use version 2 of the photocopiable page. Ask them to work individually to evaluate the film trailer. Use Snowballing to share all the ideas (children form a pair, then each pair joins with a second pair; the group of four joins another group before finally assembling all the ideas on the class whiteboard). Replay the trailer several times or allow children access to the relevant website so they can replay it as they tackle each evaluation question. Assess how well children can evaluate the contributions of sound, words and images in terms of the impact of a persuasive text.

Assessment evidence
Although this phase of work is heavily based upon Speaking and listening skills, the completed film trailer evaluation and children's oral contributions will demonstrate their ability to retrieve information from the film and to use an appropriate and effective selection of vocabulary when writing. This activity will provide evidence against Reading AF2 and Writing AF7.

Next steps
Support: Provide children with a bank of adjective cards (for example: funny, sad, frightening, scared, and intrigued). Discuss the meaning of all the cards before asking questions about the trailer: *What was the music like? How did the clips make you feel?* Children can then select a card that reflects their response. Ask them why they chose that card. Help them to relate their answer to examples from the trailer.
Extension: Source suitable film trailer reviews on the internet (print off for use to avoid encounter with possible unsuitable material). Challenge children to write a critic's review of the trailer they have seen.

Key aspects of learning
Information processing: Children locate and refer to relevant examples from a DVD text.
Reasoning: Children will be able to give reasons for their opinions about the impact of a range of persuasive texts.

Phase ② Rhetorical questions

Learning outcome
Children can use key language features to plan a persuasive text.

Success criteria
● I can identify the meaning of a rhetorical question.
● I can write rhetorical questions.

Setting the context
Explain the definition of a rhetorical question and provide examples. Explain that this is a device commonly used by advertisers when they wish to evoke a particular emotional response. Give the children either the photocopiable page 'Rhetorical questions' or the interactive activity 'Rhetorical questions' and ask them to match the different rhetorical questions to the response that the advertiser intended.

Assessment opportunity
Following the matching activity the children can then write three rhetorical questions of their own using the final images on the photocopiable page as a stimulus. Assess whether children use suitable vocabulary in their writing.

Unit 4 **Persuasive texts**

Assessment evidence
At levels 2-3, children will use simple vocabulary when writing their own rhetorical questions. Some words may be selected for effect. At levels 4-5, children will incorporate use of wider vocabulary in their rhetorical questions. This activity provides evidence against Writing AF7.

Next steps
Support: Present children with an emotive picture such as a beautiful beach. Ask them how it makes them feel. What would they do there? (Relax, dive in the water…) Ask them to imagine that they are a tour operator wanting people to book holidays to go there. What questions would they ask to make people imagine they were on the beach having fun? *Can you imagine diving into the crystal clear waters of the Pacific Ocean?*
Extension: Encourage children to practise writing different types of persuasive sentences. Can they write emotive sentences using powerful adjectives?

Key aspects of learning
Reasoning: Children will be able to give reasons for their opinions about the impact of a range of persuasive texts.

Phase ② Planning a movie trailer

Learning outcome
Children can use key language features to plan a persuasive text.

Success criteria
● I can select four clips from a movie to create a film trailer.
● I can say what impact I want the soundtrack to have.
● I can say what impact I want the voice-over script to have.
● I can say what impact I want the images to have.
● I can order the clips to build tension or interest.

Setting the context
Select a suitable children's film as the subject for a film trailer. Ideally allow the children to watch the film as a whole class. Set the scene: the film has been made but has not yet been released into the cinema. The class are to be the film company's advertising board and their job is to plan a trailer to release before the film hits the cinemas with the aim of encouraging as many people to come and see the film as possible. Share the success criteria and display them so the children can refer to them during the activity.

Assessment opportunity
Arrange the children in groups of around four and give them the photocopiable page 'Film trailer planning sheet'. They will have to decide upon the intended audience and the emotional impact they wish the trailer to have on the audience. They will also decide which four clips from the film they will use and why. They can then decide whether they will include a 'hook' to encourage the viewer to want to find out what happens and state what this hook will be. They decide whether they will use a soundtrack and what impact they want this to have. Circulate round the groups listening to the contributions made by children. Assess their understanding of the function of persuasive texts and their ability to select appropriate and effective vocabulary (record observations on target children). Gather in the completed sheets at the end of the session.

Assessment evidence
At levels 2-3 children will use simple vocabulary when planning their film trailer. Some use of adventurous word choices may be evident. At levels 4-5, children will incorporate use of wider vocabulary in their planning and their ideas will be appropriate to task. This activity will gather evidence against Writing AF7.

Next steps
Support: Provide children with a teaching assistant as the director for the group. The director will help children to capture their ideas onto a shared planning sheet.
Extension: Children can take on the role of director and assimilate the group's individual ideas into a final plan.

Key aspects of learning
Information processing: Children locate and refer to relevant examples from a DVD text.
Communication: Children will develop their ability to discuss as they work collaboratively in pairs, groups and whole-class contexts. They will communicate persuasively orally, in writing and through ICT if appropriate.

Phase ③ Writing the movie trailer

Learning outcome
Children can write a persuasive text using informal language and a range of simple connectives.

Success criteria
- I can write a script for my movie trailer voice-over.
- I can add sound effects.
- I can explain the kind of music I need to add to build tension or interest.

Setting the context
This activity assumes that children have carried out the previous activity. Having previously planned their film trailer in groups of four, children will have gained an understanding of how they want their trailer to work. Hand out copies of the photocopiable page 'Voice-over script'. Tell the children to select one of the film clips and to write a voice-over in the form of a playscript independently. They should include rhetorical questions, emotive and boastful language ('the funniest movie...') as well as sound patterns and any other persuasive devices that they have encountered during the course of the unit.

Assessment opportunity
After writing individually, ask children to return to their groups from the previous activity. Ask them to take turns in reading aloud their voice-overs to the rest of the group. The group members will listen to each presentation and will evaluate the content. Children will peer-assess each other's work by providing positive feedback to every group member. They should then select an element from every group member's text to use in their 'company' voice-over. Assess the children's level of understanding regarding effective persuasive language devices. Have they adopted the form and style of the text type when writing their voice-overs?

Assessment evidence
At levels 2–3, children will make attempts to adopt an appropriate style and form in their writing. At levels 4–5, children will maintain the reader's interest in their voice-over text. The activity will provide evidence towards Writing AF2.

Next steps
Support: Provide children with a wordbank containing emotive and boastful language to help them to improve their voice-over scripts.
Extension: Children work in mixed-ability groups providing and receiving support from each other in the group situation.

Key aspects of learning
Information processing: Children locate and refer to relevant examples from a DVD text.
Communication: Children will develop their ability to discuss as they work collaboratively in pairs, groups and whole-class contexts. They will communicate persuasively orally, in writing and through ICT if appropriate.

NON-FICTION

Periodic assessment

Reading

Learning outcome Children can identify key language features in paper-based persuasive texts.	**Success criteria** I can identify the key features of a persuasive text. **Setting the context** Ask the children to read the introduction to the RSPB Youth website homepage (www.rspb.org.uk/youth/) or alternatively use the photocopiable page 'Non-fiction 4 Reading assessment text'. They will then answer a range of questions that require them to explore and interpret the text in detail to identify the persuasive features of the text. **Assessment opportunity** Give all the children the photocopiable page 'Non-fiction 4 Reading assessment'. They are required to identify persuasive devices in the text (the RSPB Youth website homepage) and make reference to them. All children can work independently to complete this activity. Gather in the completed sheets at the end of the session. **Assessment evidence** This activity will provide evidence against Reading AF4 and AF6. Use this activity as well as examples of the children's learning throughout this unit to assess their overall progress in Reading.

Writing

Learning outcome Children can write a persuasive text using informal language and a range of devices used to persuade.	**Success criteria** ● I can design a poster for a film. ● I can include strong punctuation. ● I can include a rhetorical question. ● I can include boastful phrases. ● I can include an emotive phrase or sentence. ● I can include a strong image. **Setting the context** Using the same film that the children worked on for their movie trailer (see activity on page 137), the children are now going to design a cinema poster to advertise the film. Recap all the features of persuasive writing covered during the unit. Look at a number of posters to provide stimulation and support. Allow children to use ICT to select an image to use for their poster. **Assessment opportunity** As the children plan their poster, ask them to explain each feature they have included in their poster. What impact are they hoping to achieve? Why have they chosen a specific word? Gather in the posters at the end of the activity for assessment. **Assessment evidence** This activity will provide evidence against Writing AF2 and AF7. Use the completed posters as well as samples of the children's work throughout this unit to make levels judgement for their Writing.

Advertisement (a)

③

THIS GREAT KEYRING IS YOURS FREE WHEN YOUR FRIENDS JOIN YOUNG REDWINGS!

If you pass this magazine to a friend and they join Young Redwings as a result of your recommendation, we'll send you this fab **Chrome Redwings Keyring** as a thank you. To get your free keyring your friend needs to join Young Redwings using the joining form shown here. **We look forward to hearing from your friends soon!**

cut along dashed line

Please can I join Young Redwings...

My Name:

My Date of Birth:

My Address:

Postcode:

Email Address:

I was recommended to join Young Redwings by:

Name:

Address:

Postcode:

Return to: Young Redwings Co-ordinators, Redwings Horse Sanctuary, Hapton, Norwich, NR15 1SP

rescue me...
and we did!

Piebald cob **Twiggy** was found abandoned on a busy main road in the South of England by a kind member of the public who immediately contacted a local horse watch scheme. They asked Redwings to attend and our local field officer went along, where she found a very thin and frightened pony who seemed to have an injured hip.

Twiggy
(*Ed's Note – Read more about our vet team on pages 4 and 5!)

Twiggy's owner could not be found so the local vets asked Redwings to take care of her and we very carefully transported her to the Ada Cole Rescue Centre in Essex so she didn't have to travel too far. We did some tests to make sure her hip was ok and gave her lots of yummy food to help her put on weight. Twiggy made such a good recovery that eventually she was ready to make the journey to our Horse Hospital in Norfolk. Once she had arrived safely the Redwings vet team* ran some tests to make sure her hip wasn't causing her any pain and they found that she must have had a bad injury in the past but she had become used to it and it wasn't causing her any pain now.

Lovely Twiggy is only three years old and although she will never be able to be ridden because of her hip, she will be able to live safely here at Redwings where no one will be able to frighten her ever again.

Text © 2008, Redwings Horse Sanctuary.

Advertisement (b)

how to make an innocent smoothie

squeeze one of these

over lots of these

wait for a bit

nearly there

bingo

innocent smoothies. nothing but nothing but fruit

and a nice long sleep in a field

join our family at www.innocentdrinks.co.uk/rfamily

Non-fiction 4 Reading assessment text

- Kids!
- For Teens
- Make 'n' do
- Play
- Learn
- Discover
- Join in

- Plant! (Cymraeg)
- Chwarae
- Dysgu

Welcome to RSPB Kids!

If you like birds and wildlife you've come to the right website. These pages are full of fun and facts – so don't waste time, start exploring the site!

If you're a teacher, parent or youth leader, we've included information especially for you on some of the pages.

Wildlife action awards

This award scheme is all about finding out about wildlife, doing practical things to help and telling other people. It's easy to take part and it's fun, so what are you waiting for?

Aren't birds of prey brilliant

Find out more about the birds of prey that make the UK their home, and download our fun activities for you to do at home, or at school.

Wildsquare

Choose a place you like and we will help you find out more about it. If you've not yet joined in the fun, get to know the plants, insects, birds and animals living in your local area with our exciting project.

Rainham Marshes appeal

Children and young people have a great chance to help water voles and other wildlife at our Rainham Marshes reserve. Will you help us raise money to save a special place?

POETRY
UNIT 1 Creating images

Literacy objectives

Speak and listen for a wide range of purposes in different contexts
Strand 1 Speaking
- Respond appropriately to the contributions of others in the light of differing viewpoints.

Read and write for a range of purposes on paper and on screen
Strand 6 Word structure and spelling
- Use knowledge of phonics, morphology and etymology to spell new and unfamiliar words.
Strand 7 Understanding and interpreting texts
- Explain how writers use figurative and expressive language to create images and atmosphere.
Strand 8 Engaging with and responding to texts
- Read extensively favourite authors or genres and experiment with other types of text.
- Interrogate texts to deepen and clarify understanding and response.
- Explore why and how writers write.
Strand 9 Creating and shaping texts
- Develop and refine ideas in writing using planning and problem-solving strategies.
- Choose and combine words, images and other features for particular effects.
Strand 12 Presentation
- Write consistently with neat, legible and joined handwriting.

Key aspects of learning

Information processing
- Children will explore and tease out ideas, thoughts and feelings communicated through the language and forms of poetry.
Evaluation
- Children will share their own writing outcomes, as well as those of others. They will discuss success criteria, give feedback to others and judge the effectiveness of their own work.
Reasoning
- Children will identify, explore and generate the mental connections represented by various forms of simple imagery - for example simile - a vital aspect of thinking, reasoning and understanding.
Empathy
- In discussing and writing about the poems and their images, children will need to imagine themselves in another person's position.
Self-awareness
- Children will discuss and reflect on their personal responses to the texts.
Communication
- Children will develop their ability to discuss effective communication in respect of both the language and content of poetry they are reading and writing. They will sometimes work collaboratively in pairs and in groups. They will communicate outcomes orally, and in writing and through use of ICT if appropriate.

Assessment focuses

Reading
AF4 (*identify and comment on the structure and organisation of texts, including grammatical and presentational features at text level*).
AF5 (*explain and comment on writers' use of language, including grammatical and literary features at word and sentence level*).
AF6 (*identify and comment on writers' purposes and viewpoints, and the overall effect of the text on the reader*).

Writing
AF7 (*select appropriate and effective vocabulary*).
Handwriting and presentation

Speaking and listening
Speaking (speak with clarity, intonation and pace).

Resources

Phase 1 activities
Photocopiable page, 'Greengrocer'
Photocopiable page, 'Greengrocer – poem analysis'
Photocopiable page, 'Analysis record sheet'
Photocopiable page, 'Poems that create images'
Interactive activity, 'Creating images'
Phase 2 activities
Photocopiable page, 'Images of the Moon' (versions 1 and 2)
Phase 3 activities
Photocopiable page, 'Sea Seasons'
Photocopiable page, 'My sea poem' (versions 1 and 2)
Periodic assessment
Photocopiable page, 'Poetry 1 Reading assessment text'
Photocopiable page, 'Poetry 1 Reading assessment'
Photocopiable page, 'Poetry 1 Writing assessment (a)'
Photocopiable page, 'Poetry 1 Writing assessment (b)'

Unit 1 📖 Creating images

Learning outcomes	Assessment opportunity and evidence	Assessment focuses (AFs)		Success criteria
		Level 2	Level 3	
Phase ① activities pages 148–149				
Imagery in poems Children can recognise and discuss how poets use language to create a vivid picture in words.	● Supported discussion groups where children read and analyse poems. ● Children's oral responses and teacher's notes.	**Reading AF5** ● Some effective language choices noted. ● Some familiar patterns of language identified.	**Reading AF5** A few basic features of writer's use of language identified, but with little or no comment.	● I can identify similes in a poem. ● I can explain how the language in a poem is creating images.
Favourite poems Children have increased the range of poetry of which they are aware and can discuss likes and dislikes with reasons.	● Paired discussion where children read and analyse poems. ● Children's oral responses.	**Reading AF6** ● Some awareness that writers have viewpoints and purposes. ● Simple statements about likes and dislikes in reading, sometimes with reasons.	**Reading AF6** ● Comments identify main purpose. ● Express personal response but with little awareness of writer's viewpoint or effect on reader.	● I can select a favourite poem and say why I liked it. ● I can compare poems by the same author.
Phase ② activities page 150				
What is the Moon like? Children understand how to plan and write a poem based on a model using similes and powerful verbs and adverbs to create images.	● Independent activity where children write their own poems. ● Children's completed brainstorming sheets and finished poems.	**Reading AF4** Some awareness of use of features of organisation. **Writing AF7** ● Simple, often speech-like vocabulary conveys relevant meanings. ● Some adventurous word choices.	**Reading AF4** A few basic features of organisation at text level identified, with little or no linked comment. **Writing AF7** ● Simple, generally appropriate vocabulary used, limited in range. ● Some words selected for effect or occasion.	● I can plan and write a poem based on a model. ● I can use similes in my poem. ● I can use powerful verbs in my poem.
Phase ③ activities pages 151–152				
Choosing words for effect Children can write their own simple poem based on one previously read and analysed.	● Independent activity where children analyse the poem, *Sea Seasons* and write three more verses. ● Children's analysis sheets and poems.	**Reading AF4** Some awareness of use of features of organisation. **Writing AF7** ● Simple, often speech-like vocabulary conveys relevant meanings. ● Some adventurous word choices.	**Reading AF4** A few basic features of organisation at text level identified, with little or no linked comment. **AF7 In most writing** ● Simple, generally appropriate vocabulary used, limited in range. ● Some words selected for effect or occasion.	● I can use a poem to create a writing template and then use the template to write my own poem. ● I can use similes to create powerful images. ● I can use powerful verbs and adverbs for effect.
Class anthology Children can present their work using neat, legible handwriting in a cursive style.	● Independent activity where children write up their draft poems in the cursive style of handwriting. ● Children's poems.	**Handwriting and presentation** ● Letters generally correctly shaped but inconsistencies in orientation, size and use of upper/lower case letters. ● Clear letter formation, with ascenders and descenders distinguished, generally upper and lower case letters not mixed within words.	**Handwriting and presentation** Legible style shows accurate and consistent letter formation, sometimes joined.	I can use neat, joined handwriting to present my work.

Unit 1 ◻ Creating images

Learning outcomes	Assessment opportunity and evidence	Assessment focuses (AFs)		Success criteria
		Level 4	Level 5	
Phase ① activities pages 148–149				
Imagery in poems Children can recognise and discuss how poets use language to create a vivid picture in words.	• Discussion groups where children read and analyse poems. • Children's oral responses and teacher's notes.	**Reading AF5** • Some basic features of writer's use of language identified. • Simple comments on writer's choices.	**Reading AF5** • Various features of writer's use of language identified, with some explanation. • Comments show some awareness of the effect of writer's language choices.	• I can identify similes in a poem. • I can explain how the language in a poem is creating images.
Favourite poems Children have increased the range of poetry of which they are aware and can discuss likes and dislikes with reasons.	• Paired discussion where children read and analyse poems. • Children's oral responses.	**Reading AF6** • Main purpose identified. • Simple comments show some awareness of writer's viewpoint. • Simple comment on overall effect on reader.	**Reading AF6** • Main purpose clearly identified, often through general overview. • Viewpoint in texts clearly identified, with some, often limited, explanation. • General awareness of effect on the reader, with some, often limited, explanation.	• I can select a favourite poem and say why I liked it. • I can compare poems by the same author.
Phase ② activities page 150				
What is the Moon like? Children understand how to plan and write a poem based on a model using similes and powerful verbs and adverbs to create images.	• Independent activity where children write their own poems. • Children's completed brainstorming sheets and finished poems.	**Reading AF4** Some basic features of organisation at text level identified. **Writing AF7** • Some evidence of deliberate vocabulary choices. • Some expansion of general vocabulary to match topic.	**Reading AF4** Various features relating to organisation at text level, including form, are clearly identified, with some explanation. **Writing AF7** • Vocabulary chosen for effect. • Reasonably wide vocabulary used, though not always appropriately.	• I can plan and write a poem based on a model. • I can use similes in my poem. • I can use powerful verbs in my poem.
Phase ③ activities pages 151–152				
Choosing words for effect Children can write their own simple poem based on one previously read and analysed.	• Independent activity where children analyse the poem, *Sea Seasons* and write three more verses. • Children's analysis sheets and poems.	**Reading AF4** Some basic features of organisation at text level identified. **Writing AF7** • Some evidence of deliberate vocabulary choices. • Some expansion of general vocabulary to match topic.	**Reading AF4** Various features relating to organisation at text level, including form, are clearly identified, with some explanation. **Writing AF7** • Vocabulary chosen for effect. • Reasonably wide vocabulary used, though not always appropriately.	• I can use a poem to create a writing template and then use the template to write my own poem. • I can use similes to create powerful images. • I can use powerful verbs and adverbs for effect.
Class anthology Children can present their work using neat, legible handwriting in a cursive style.	• Independent activity where children write up their draft poems in the cursive style of handwriting. • Children's hand-written poems.	**Level 3 Handwriting and presentation** Legible style shows accurate and consistent letter formation, sometimes joined.	**Level 3 Handwriting and presentation** Legible style shows accurate and consistent letter formation, sometimes joined.	I can use neat, joined handwriting to present my work.

POETRY

Phase ① Imagery in poems

Learning outcome
Children can recognise and discuss how poets use language to create a vivid picture in words.

Success criteria
- I can identify similes in a poem.
- I can explain how the language in a poem is creating images.

Setting the context
This activity should be carried out once the children have been taught the definition of a simile and have had practice identifying them. More confident learners may be aware of the term 'metaphor'. Ensure everyone knows what a greengrocer is and check that the children have all seen a greengrocer's shop. Discuss how the fruit and vegetables are all set out in boxes. If they do not know what a greengrocer's is like, invite them to picture the fruit and vegetables on a market stall or in a supermarket. Take photos and display them on the whiteboard. Read the poem *Greengrocer* to the class.

Assessment opportunity
Following the shared reading of the poem give each child the photocopiable page 'Greengrocer'. Put children working at levels 2–3 to work in a supported discussion group. Read a verse and then ask questions to check if children can identify similes: *What is the poet comparing a pineapple with?* (She is saying it is like a prehistoric dragon with spiny, spiky shoulders.) *Why do you think she chose to compare a pineapple with a dragon?* (because a pineapple is rough and scaly and has spiky leaves like a dragon). Act as scribe taking each verse at a time and recording individual children's responses, on the photocopiable page 'Analysis record sheet', maybe drawing each of the fruits or vegetables and annotating these with the children's comments. Ask children working at levels 4–5 to independently complete the photocopiable page 'Greengrocer – poem analysis'. As children complete the activity, they will identify similes and should explain why the poet chose that particular language to create the images.

Assessment evidence
At levels 2–3, children will be able to identify the simple similes (comparisons where the poet has used 'like') without further explanation. At levels 4–5 children will analyse each verse, stating what the fruit or vegetable is being compared to or described as and will provide an explanation in simple terms as to why the poet has chosen to make this comparison. They may include an explanation of what image the description conjures up in their mind. Children working at level 5 may also be able to distinguish between a simile and a metaphor. Their written comments will provide evidence for Reading AF5.

Next steps
Support: For those children who could not explain why the language was used to create the specific images, bring in samples of some of the fruits and vegetables and work in small discussion groups to analyse each verse further. Work on them creating similes of their own, for example, 'The potatoes lay like muddy pebbles washed up on an estuary bank when the tide is out'.
Extension: Challenge children to read through poetry anthologies and select poems containing language that creates images. Invite them to write up the poem and comment on it, and stick it in a class anthology of favourite poems. Children can then share their choice with the class.

Key aspects of learning
Information processing: Children will explore and tease out the ideas, thoughts and feelings communicated through the language and forms of poetry.
Reasoning: Children will identify, explore and generate the mental connections represented by various forms of simple imagery – for example simile – a vital aspect of thinking, reasoning and understanding.

Phase ① Favourite poems

Learning outcome
Children have increased the range of poetry of which they are aware and can discuss likes and dislikes with reasons.

Success criteria
● I can select a favourite poem and say why I liked it.
● I can compare poems by the same author.

Setting the context
Children are provided with copies of four poems that create images related to a broad theme of winter, snow, ice, the cold and so on. Give all the children a copy of the photocopiable page 'Poems that create images'. The poem *January* is a list of metaphors for the month. The language in *The Snow Monster* creates an image of an enormous monster in the sky and the effect it has on Earth when he sneezes, bellows, cries and sleeps. *Hard Winters* is a far simpler poem which compares and contrasts outside and inside on a winter's day and contains a simple simile. Finally, *What is Slippery?* is another metaphorical poem with different layers of meaning. The poems provide the opportunity for assessing the depth of analysis by children.

Assessment opportunity
Carry out the classroom discussion technique of 'Think-Pair-Share'. Ask all the children to read the four poems individually. Allow them to digest them and decide on a response to each poem - *Which created the most powerful images? Which language was the most effective? Which did you like best and why? Which poem contains a simile?* Use the interactive activity 'Creating images' to allow children to substitute words in the poem *What is Cold?* (based on *What is Slippery?*) How do their choices affect the rhythm? Do they realise different words conjure up better images? Ask the children to pair up and explain their ideas to their partner. After the pairs have discussed the issue, ask them to join another pair, to share views and to emerge with a group perspective. Circulate among the groups making notes of how children approached the task. Using a class list, record which children could give a simple expression of likes and dislikes, who could give reasons, and who could explain the writer's viewpoint and the reasoning for the language choices.

Assessment evidence
At levels 2-3, children will express their own preferences and may give simple reasons for their choices. At levels 4-5, children will express their preferences and explain why they liked the poem having considered the poet's viewpoint. They may be able to explain their preference having understood the writer's intended impact on the reader. Use these comments to provide evidence against Reading AF6.

Next steps
Support: Set up a supported guided reading group and use carefully considered dialogue to lead the children to analyse the poems.
Extension: Select a poem each week for children to take home, read and analyse and then to share and discuss in class. Keep this up as a regular end of week or start the week activity. The poems and reviews could be gathered into a class anthology.

Key aspects of learning
Information processing: Children will explore and tease out the ideas, thoughts and feelings communicated through the language and forms of poetry.
Reasoning: Children will identify, explore and generate the mental connections represented by various forms of simple imagery - for example simile - a vital aspect of thinking, reasoning and understanding.
Self-awareness: Children will discuss and reflect on their personal responses to the texts.
Communication: Children will develop their ability to discuss effective communication in respect of both the language and content of poetry they are reading and writing. They will sometimes work collaboratively in pairs and in groups. They will communicate outcomes orally, and in writing and through use of ICT if appropriate.

POETRY

Phase ② What is the Moon like?

Success criteria
- I can plan and write a poem based on a model.
- I can use similes in my poem.
- I can choose powerful verbs in my poem.

Setting the context
Invite children to visualise the Moon and to think about how it lights up the night sky, think about its different shapes, and what it does. Give children the photocopiable page 'Images of the Moon' (versions 1 or 2) and explain that this is what the poet did in order to write her poem. Read the poem together and discuss its form. Ask the children: *How does the poem start? What type of single word is on every other line? How is the simile formed?*

Assessment opportunity
Following the shared discussion ask the children to use the template on the second page of the photocopiable page 'Images of the Moon' to write a second verse in the same style. Pose questions to encourage children to consider which verbs describe what the Moon does, which nouns to compare the Moon with and which adjectives to describe the nouns. Children working at levels 2–3 can use version 1 of the photocopiable page which provides a wordbank of verbs, nouns and adjectives to assemble into similes. When children have completed their poems, refer them to the success criteria and ask them to identify where they have created similes, where they have used powerful verbs and whether the poem follows the structure of the model. Encourage reflection of word choices and ask them to find an example that they are proud of and circle it. Ask the children to find a talk partner and to carry out pair-share assessment of each other's poems. They should tell their partner why they are proud of the chosen example. Next they should decide with their partner which of the success criteria they have been most successful with and which one needs help or could be taken even further. Assess children's final poems in terms of the appropriateness of their vocabulary choices (eg use of powerful verbs), the range of vocabulary and their ability to form imaginative images (eg similes).

Assessment evidence
At levels 2–3, children will show some awareness of the structure of the poem on which they will base their own verse but with little comment. When writing their own poem they will use simple vocabulary to create similes which compare the Moon to everyday objects. At levels 4–5, children will identify and comment on the structural and organisational features of the shared poem. In their own writing they will use an expanding vocabulary that matches the topic using words which are carefully chosen for effect. This activity will provide evidence towards Reading AF4 and Writing AF7.

Next steps
Support: For children who are unable to visualise and create similes, provide pictures as a concrete stimulus. Discuss the images and use leading questions to elicit a comparison. Once a comparison is made (such as 'it looks like a ball') ask children to describe how the ball moves, what sort of ball it is, and so on, to assist in creating the image.
Extension: Encourage children to search for alternative poems about the Moon and to analyse the structure and expand on it with new ideas if possible.

Key aspects of learning
Evaluation: Children will share their own writing outcomes, as well as those of others. They will discuss success criteria, give feedback to others and judge the effectiveness of their own work.

Phase ③ Choosing words for effect

Learning outcome
Children can write their own simple poem based on one previously read and analysed.

Success criteria
● I can use a poem to create a writing template and then use the template to write my own poem.
● I can use similes to create powerful images.
● I can use powerful verbs and adverbs for effect.

Setting the context
Recap the pattern used in the poem *Images of the Moon*. Introduce *Sea Seasons* from the photocopiable page as a sequence poem that has a clear structure. Read it together before giving all children the photocopiable page 'My sea poem' (versions 1 or 2). Go through the first verse with the class, picking out all the features that are repeated and confirm understanding of terms such as preposition, alliteration, powerful verbs and noun phrases. Invite children to add a simile into each verse of the original poem at the prompt lines.

Assessment opportunity
Ask the children to work individually to annotate the remaining three verses. This will help them gain sufficient knowledge to form a template on which to base their own version of the poem. Next, encourage children to brainstorm verbs and nouns before attempting to write their poems. Provide a thesaurus for each child to work with. Ask them to find a partner and assess each other's poems. Tell them to use a highlighter to identify their favourite choice of powerful verb and their favourite simile, and then to provide a 'wish' which should be a suggestion for improving a specific aspect of the poem. Assess the children on their ability to recognise features of organisation of the text and how they use this to write their own poem. Provide less confident learners with a bank of appropriate words. The similes and powerful verbs they choose to create a sequenced image of the sea through the seasons will allow you an insight into their vocabulary.

Assessment evidence
At levels 2-3, children will select and use simple vocabulary to describe what the sea is like. They will also demonstrate some awareness of features of organisation. At levels 4-5, children will use a more expansive vocabulary that matches the topic. They may use a thesaurus independently to select and widen their vocabulary choices. They will be able to mirror the structure of the original poem. The completed photocopiable page will provide evidence against Reading AF4 and the poems will provide evidence against Writing AF7.

Next steps
Support: Children who need support could use a simplified format to write their poem. For example, they could describe what a fruit tree looks like in each season: the blossom in spring, the leaves in summer, the fruit in autumn and the bare branches in winter.
Extension: Children could use the poem structure to write similar poems using other subjects in nature such as the wind or rain. More confident learners could extend their imaging further to incorporate personification.

Key aspects of learning
Evaluation: Children will share their own writing outcomes, as well as those of others. They will discuss success criteria, give feedback to others and judge the effectiveness of their own work.
Reasoning: Children will identify, explore and generate the mental connections represented by various forms of simple imagery - for example simile - a vital aspect of thinking, reasoning and understanding.
Empathy: In discussing and writing about the poems and their images, children will need to imagine themselves in another person's position.
Self-awareness: Children will discuss and reflect on their personal responses to the texts.

POETRY

Phase ③ Class anthology

Learning outcome
Children can present their work using neat, legible handwriting in a cursive style.

Success criteria
I can use neat, joined handwriting to present my work.

Setting the context
Use an oversized A4 project book as a means of creating a class anthology of poems. Explain to the children that their work is to be published and the anthology circulated around the other classes in order that their work can be celebrated around the school. Explain that you will be assessing handwriting and will be looking for a neat, cursive style with appropriate illustrations. For children who are already working at a high level 3 for handwriting you may prefer to use this opportunity for directed work such as guided reading with a teaching assistant.

Assessment opportunity
Ask the children to write up, by hand, the poem that they produced in the previous activity. Take this opportunity to observe the children's letter formation and their ability to adopt a cursive style. Record the names of the children who may be starting letters in the wrong place as this will hinder their ability to progress to a cursive style. These children may require some extra small group work with a teaching assistant to practise letter formation.

Assessment evidence
Handwriting and presentation can be assessed and evidence recorded up to level 3. Children who are a secure level 3 in handwriting will adopt a legible style of handwriting that is sometimes joined and will demonstrate consistent letter formation. Note which children are secure and which children have not yet achieved this level.

Next steps
Support: Identify those children who are not using a cursive style and provide support exercises to take home. Assess the joins that are not present and use an online writing program for practice.
Extension: Extend children by encouraging them to adopt specific handwriting styles for presentation work.

Key aspects of learning
Communication: Children will develop their ability to discuss effective communication in respect of both the language and content of poetry they are reading and writing. They will sometimes work collaboratively in pairs and in groups. They will communicate outcomes orally, and in writing and through ICT if appropriate.

Periodic assessment

Reading

Learning outcome
Children will recognise and discuss how poets use language (including similes and metaphors and other simple images) to create a vivid picture in words.

Success criteria
- I can explain how the language in a poem is creating images.
- I can identify similes in a poem.
- I can identify metaphors in a poem.

Setting the context
Deserted Greenhouse by Moira Andrew is a collection of images, created using carefully chosen words, which are placed within a picture of an abandoned greenhouse. The images are a collection of more complex similes and metaphors than the children have so far encountered during the assessment activities. The poem provides a model and a format for building images. Some of the vocabulary will require explanation before children read and analyse the images ('dowager', 'favours', 'phoenix', 'detritus', 'defeated', 'withered', 'forlorn' and 'abandoned'). Display and discuss the success criteria and explain that children are going to work using the Think-pair-share technique to read and analyse *Deserted Greenhouse*.

Assessment opportunity
Give all the children a copy of the poem *Deserted Greenhouse* from the photocopiable page 'Poetry 1 Reading assessment text' and the photocopiable page 'Poetry 1 Reading assessment'. Ask them to read the poem, then pair up and discuss it, recording their ideas on the sheet. Then ask each pair to then pair up with a second pair to share and develop their thoughts. Children working at level 2 can work in a guided group led by an adult. Each group will then feed back to the class with their responses. Explain that you will be circulating among the pairs and groups and listening and responding to their dialogue to enable you to judge their understanding and learning, and so assess where they need help to develop and improve their ability to meet the success criteria. The use of structured dialogue will enable the children to develop their own learning. Through talk they will become aware of their own learning needs and develop pathways to improvement. Make notes on children's understandings and misconceptions that evolve during the dialogue session to inform the next steps in their learning during the next Poetry Unit 2 'Exploring form'.

Assessment evidence
Your notes on the children's oral responses will provide evidence against Reading AF4, AF5 and AF6. Use this activity as well as examples of children's work throughout this unit to make level judgements for Reading.

Periodic assessment

Writing

Learning outcome
Children can paint a vivid word picture using similes and other simple images.

Success criteria
● I can write a poem which uses similes.
● I can write a poem which uses metaphors.
● I can write a poem which uses powerful verbs.
● I can write a poem which creates a powerful image in the mind of the reader.

Setting the context
Explain to the class that they are going to create a mural poem in the same style as *Deserted Greenhouse*. Suggest ideas for the mural such as an underground station at rush hour, a busy street scene, a shipwreck, a scrap-yard or a supermarket: choose the setting which is most appropriate for your class. Search for images to act as a stimulus on the internet. Children will use the photocopiable pages 'Poetry 1 Writing assessment (a)' and 'Poetry 1 Writing assessment (b)' to record their ideas and formulate them into images. The images can then be shared, reviewed and edited as part of the assessment process and amalgamated into a class mural that can then be illustrated and displayed.

Assessment opportunity
Ask the children to record what they would actually see in the chosen scene. Invite them to create similes or metaphors to describe each image – being selective about their choice of verbs, adjectives and adverbs. Direct them to use a thesaurus to help with vocabulary choices. The children should then carry out self-assessment of their ideas against the success criteria and choose their favourite image to share with the class. Record the ideas on the board and as a class celebrate each idea: 'That's a great image, I like the way you have...' and 'That is an excellent verb to describe how...' Remind the children to refer back to the success criteria to enable them to assess the quality of their work.

Assessment evidence
The level and breadth of vocabulary used and the ability to create images using similes will indicate the level at which children are working at the end of this unit. Assess their vocabulary choices against Writing AF7. Each child's verbal contribution and individual planning sheet can be used to gather evidence against Writing AF7. Use this activity and examples of children's work throughout this unit to make level judgements in Writing.

Greengrocer

The greengrocer
stands guard over
heaped-up hoards
of jewelled treasure.

Blackcurrants,
purple as amethyst,
are piled berry on
berry in boxes.

Raspberries
huddle together
like broken beads,
packed into baskets.

Cherries light
round red lamps,
flaring rubies
on dark shelves.

Strawberries jostle
cheek to cheek,
juice seeping from
freckled faces.

With toothless
wide yellow smiles,
bananas laugh at
their own jokes.

Like prehistoric
dragons, pineapples
shrug their spiny
spiky shoulders.

Oranges open their
round mouths,
crying 'O' like the
Man-in-the-moon.

Round, golden
as summer suns,
grapefruit glow from
bright shiny skins.

Red apples lie in
blue beds, snuggling
together like netted
billiard balls.

Carrots rudely point
orange fingers at
the floor, their green
hair tangled in knots.

Potatoes, piled like
stones in sacks, gaze
unglamorously from
mud-covered faces.

Framed in green
curtains, cauliflowers
frown from curled
tissue-paper eyes.

Wearing brown
skin-tight trousers,
troubled onions sit
holding back tears.

Leeks, in long
green stockings,
dangle white hairy
feet from the shelves.

Peas, cradled in pods,
keep their emeralds
hidden until a thumb
unlocks the caskets.

The greengrocer
counts his takings,
sighs, closing the lid
on a treasure chest.

Moira Andrew

Name   Date

POETRY

Greengrocer – poem analysis

Name of fruit or vegetable	What it is compared to	Why I think the poet made this comparison
Raspberries	Broken beads	The segments of raspberries look like they are broken.

Red
Amber
Green

I can identify similes in a poem. ☐

I can explain how the language in a poem is creating images. ☐

Name	Date

Poems that create images

January

January is
a clean white sheet, newly-ironed;
an empty page;
a field of freshly-fallen snow
waiting to be mapped
By our footsteps.

John Foster

Hard winters

Outside
The bare branches of trees
Shiver in the wind
And the frozen grass
Sticks up like spikes
From the hard ground.

Inside
Children with chapped hands
Stretch thin fingers
To catch wisps of warmth
From scraps of coal
Glimmering in the iron grate.

John Foster

What is slippery?

An icy puddle,
A bar of soap,
Soft ice-cream
As it slides down your throat.

A water slide,
A squirming fish,
The end of a rainbow,
A whispered wish.

Moss-covered stones,
The banks of a stream,
The glimpse of a shadow,
A fading dream.

John Foster

Text © 1997, John Foster. Illustration © Bill Houston/Bill Houston Creative Limited.

Sea seasons

The sea bounces
over barnacles,
bobbing and buckling
in the springtime breeze.

The sea slithers
across shingle,
splintering and sparkling
under a bright summer sun.

The sea prowls
over pebbles,
pimpling and prickling
on damp autumn days.

The sea rushes
across rocks,
ranting and raving
when winter winds blow.

Moira Andrew

Text © 1998, Moira Andrew. Illustration © Bill Houston/Bill Houston Creative Limited

Poetry 1 Reading assessment text

Deserted Greenhouse

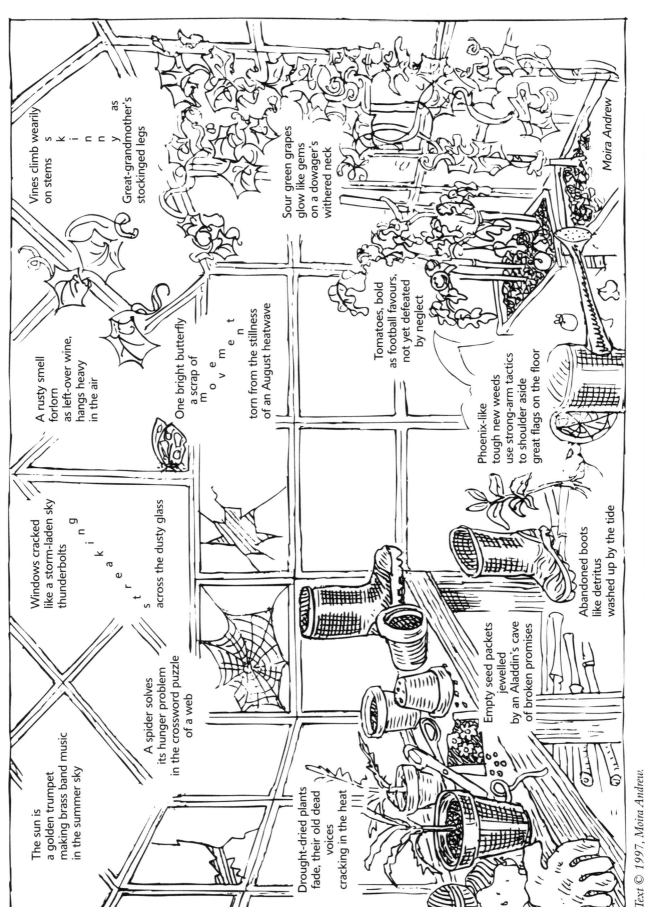

Vines climb wearily
on stems
s
k
i
n
n
y as
Great-grandmother's
stockinged legs

Sour green grapes
glow like gems
on a dowager's
withered neck

A rusty smell
forlorn
as left-over wine,
hangs heavy
in the air

One bright butterfly
a scrap of
m
o
v
e
m
e
n
t
torn from the stillness
of an August heatwave

Tomatoes, bold
as football favours,
not yet defeated
by neglect

Windows cracked
like a storm-laden sky
thunderbolts
b
r
e
a
k
i
n
g
across the dusty glass

Phoenix-like
tough new weeds
use strong-arm tactics
to shoulder aside
great flags on the floor

Abandoned boots
like detritus
washed up by the tide

A spider solves
its hunger problem
in the crossword puzzle
of a web

Empty seed packets
jewelled
by an Aladdin's cave
of broken promises

The sun is
a golden trumpet
making brass band music
in the summer sky

Drought-dried plants
fade, their old dead
voices
cracking in the heat

Moira Andrew

Text © 1997, Moira Andrew.

POETRY
UNIT 2 Exploring form

Literacy objectives

Speak and listen for a wide range of purposes in different contexts
Strand 1 Speaking
- Respond appropriately to the contributions of others in the light of differing viewpoints.

Read and write for a range of purposes on paper and on screen
Strand 7 Understanding and interpreting texts
- Explain how writers use figurative and expressive language to create images and atmosphere.
Strand 8 Engaging with and responding to texts
- Read extensively favourite authors or genres and experiment with other types of text.
- Interrogate texts to deepen and clarify understanding and response.
- Explore why and how writers write, including through face-to-face and online contact with authors.
Strand 9 Creating and shaping texts
- Choose and combine words, images and other features for particular effects.
Strand 12 Presentation
- Write consistently with neat, legible and joined handwriting.
- Use word-processing packages to present written work and continue to increase speed and accuracy in typing.

Key aspects of learning

Creative thinking
- Children will have the opportunity to respond imaginatively to the stimulus of a first-hand experience and may be able to express their response by presenting poetry through sound and image to enhance its meaning.
Self-awareness
- Children will discuss and reflect on their personal responses to the texts.
Reasoning
- Children will explain their opinions about different poems and use particular words and phrases to support or illustrate their ideas.
Evaluation
- Children will have regular opportunities to review their work against agreed success criteria. They will view their own and their peers' presentations and discuss ways to improve them.
Social skills
- When designing group presentations, children will learn about relating to the other group members effectively.
Communication
- Children will often work collaboratively in pairs and groups. They will communicate outcomes orally, in writing and through ICT.

Assessment focuses

Reading

AF1 (*use a range of strategies, including accurate decoding of text, to read for meaning*).
AF4 (*identify and comment on the structure and organisation of texts, including grammatical and presentational features at text level*).
AF5 (*explain and comment on writers' use of language, including grammatical and literary features at word and sentence level*).
AF6 (*identify and comment on writers' purposes and viewpoints and the overall effect of the text on the reader*).

Writing

AF1 (*write imaginative, interesting and thoughtful texts*).
AF3 (*organise and present whole texts effectively, sequencing and structuring information, ideas and events*).

Speaking and listening

Speaking (speak with clarity, intonation and pace).

Resources

Phase 1 activities
Photocopiable page, 'Haiku, tanka and cinquain'
Photocopiable page, 'Features of poems'
Photocopiable page, 'Cat poems (a)'
Photocopiable page, 'Cat poems (b)'
Photocopiable page, 'Cat poems (c)'
Photocopiable page, 'Cat poems (d)'
Phase 2 activities
Photocopiable page, 'My cat haiku'
Recording software such as Windows® Sound Recorder; microphones; PowerPoint® or similar presentation program; images for use in presentations; internet access
Phase 3 activities
Photocopiable page, 'Presentation feedback'
Periodic assessment
Photocopiable page, 'Poetry 2 Reading assessment'
Photocopiable page, 'Poetry 2 Writing assessment'

Unit 2 ☐ Exploring form

Learning outcomes	Assessment opportunity and evidence	Assessment focuses (AFs)		Success criteria
		Level 2	Level 3	

Phase ① activities pages 165-167

Haiku, tanka and cinquain Children listen for and use some technical terms in discussion of poems.	• Independent activity where children count syllables in poems in order to identify the nature of the poem. • Completed photocopiable pages.	**Reading AF4** Some awareness of use of features of organisation.	**Reading AF4** A few basic features of organisation at text level identified, with little or no linked comment.	• I can count and show syllables in words. • I can identify a haiku. • I can identify a tanka poem. • I can identify a cinquain poem.
Features of poems Children can understand how the use of expressive and descriptive language can create effects or generate emotional responses.	• Whole-class activity where children highlight specific features of a poem and discuss its overall impact. • Children's annotations and oral responses to questions.	**Reading AF6** • Some awareness that writers have viewpoints and purposes. • Simple statements about likes and dislikes in reading, sometimes with reasons.	**Reading AF6** • Comments identify main purpose. • Express personal response but with little awareness of writer's viewpoint or effect on reader.	• I can identify different features in a poem which create an emotional response. • I can recognise how a poem is performed to create an impact.
Reading out loud Children can experiment orally with phrases and words to create different effects and responses.	• Groups activity where children perform one of the chosen poems. • Children's performances and teacher's observations.	**Reading AF1** • Range of key words read on sight. • Unfamiliar words decoded using appropriate strategies. • Some fluency and expression.	**Reading AF1** Range of strategies used mostly effectively to read with fluency, understanding and expression.	• I can perform a poem out loud with expression, change of tone and volume.

Phase ② activities pages 167-169

| **Writing a poem** Children can write their own haiku poem. | • Independent activity where children write a haiku. • Peer evaluation • Children's finished poems. | **Writing AF1** • Mostly relevant ideas and content, sometimes repetitive or sparse. • Some apt word choices create interest. • Brief comments, questions about events or actions suggest viewpoint. | **Writing AF1** • Some appropriate ideas and content included. • Some attempt to elaborate on basic information or events. • Attempt to adopt viewpoint, though often not maintained or inconsistent. | • I can write a haiku. |
| **Poetry presentation** Children can plan, organise and create an ICT-based poetry presentation that involves each member of the group. | • Groups activity where children record performances of their poems and combine their recordings with text and supporting images and sound clips. • PowerPoint® presentations. | **Writing AF3** Some basic sequencing of ideas or material. | **Writing AF3** • Some attempt to organise ideas with related points placed next to each other. • Some attempt to sequence ideas or material logically. | I can combine words, images and sounds to create an effective poetry presentation. |

Unit 2 ⬜ Exploring form

Learning outcomes	Assessment opportunity and evidence	Assessment focuses (AFs)		Success criteria
		Level 2	Level 3	
Phase ③ activities pages 169				
Evaluating the presentation Children can reflect on and evaluate the quality of their peers' poetry presentations.	● Group activity where children evaluate another groups' performance. ● Children's completed sheets and verbal comments.	**Reading AF6** ● Some awareness that writers have viewpoints and purposes. ● Simple statements about likes and dislikes in reading, sometimes with reasons.	**Reading AF6** ● Comments identify main purpose. ● Express personal response but with little awareness of writer's viewpoint or effect on reader.	I can comment constructively on the work of others.

Learning outcomes	Assessment opportunity and evidence	Assessment focuses (AFs)		Success criteria
		Level 4	Level 5	
Phase ① activities pages 165-167				
Haiku, tanka and cinquain Children listen for and use some technical terms when discussing poems.	● Independent activity where children count syllables in poems in order to identify the nature of the poem. ● Completed photocopiable pages.	**Reading AF4** ● Some structural choices identified with simple comment. ● Some basic features of organisation at text level identified.	**Reading AF4** ● Comments on structural choices show some general awareness of author's craft. ● Various features relating to organisation at text level, including form, are clearly identified, with some explanation.	● I can count and show syllables in words. ● I can identify a haiku. ● I can identify a tanka poem. ● I can identify a cinquain poem.
Features of poems Children can understand how the use of expressive and descriptive language can create effects or generate emotional responses.	● Whole-class activity where children highlight specific features of a poem and discuss its overall impact. ● Children's annotations and oral responses to questions.	**Reading AF6** ● Main purpose identified. ● Simple comments show some awareness of writer's viewpoint. ● Simple comment on overall effect on reader.	**Reading AF6** ● Main purpose clearly identified, often through general overview. ● Viewpoint in texts clearly identified, with some, often limited, explanation. ● General awareness of effect on the reader, with some, often limited, explanation.	● I can identify different features in a poem which create an emotional response. ● I can recognise how a poem is performed to create an impact.
Reading out loud Children can experiment orally with phrases and words to create different effects and responses.	● Groups activity where children perform one of the chosen poems. ● Children's performances and teacher's observations.	**Level 3 Reading AF1** Range of strategies used mostly effectively to read with fluency, understanding and expression.	**Level 3 Reading AF1** Range of strategies used mostly effectively to read with fluency, understanding and expression.	I can perform a poem out loud with expression, change of tone and volume.
Phase ② activities pages 167-169				
Writing a poem Children can write their own haiku poem.	● Independent activity where children write a haiku. ● Peer evaluation. ● Children's finished poems.	**Writing AF1** ● Relevant ideas and content chosen. ● Some ideas and material developed in detail. ● Straightforward viewpoint generally established and maintained.	**Writing AF1** ● Relevant ideas and material developed with some imaginative detail. ● Development of ideas and material appropriately shaped for selected form. ● Clear viewpoint established, generally consistent, with some elaboration.	I can write a haiku.

POETRY

Learning outcomes	Assessment opportunity and evidence	Assessment focuses (AFs)		Success criteria
		Level 4	Level 5	
Poetry presentation Children can plan, organise and create an ICT-based poetry presentation that involves each member of the group.	• Group activity where children record performances of their poems and combine their recordings with text, supporting images and sound clips. • PowerPoint® presentations.	**Writing AF3** • Ideas organised by clustering related points or by time sequence. • Ideas are organised simply with a fitting opening and closing. • Ideas or material generally in logical sequence but over-all direction of writing not always clearly signalled.	**Writing AF3** • Material is structured clearly, with sentence organised into appropriate paragraphs. • Development of material is effectively managed across text. • Overall direction of the text supported by clear links between paragraphs.	I can combine words, images and sounds to create an effective poetry presentation.

Phase ③ activities page 169

Evaluating the presentation Children can reflect on and evaluate the quality of their peers' poetry presentations.	• Group activity where children evaluate another groups' performance. • Children's completed sheets and verbal comments.	**Reading AF6** • Main purpose identified. • Simple comments show some awareness of writer's viewpoint. • Simple comment on overall effect on reader.	**Reading AF6** • Main purpose clearly identified, often through general overview. • Viewpoint in texts clearly identified, with some, often limited, explanation. • General awareness of effect on the reader, with some, often limited, explanation.	I can comment constructively on the work of others.

Phase ① Haiku, tanka and cinquain

Learning outcome
Children listen for and use some technical terms in discussion of poems.

Success criteria
- I can count and show syllables in words.
- I can identify a traditional haiku.
- I can identify a tanka poem.
- I can identify a cinquain poem.

Setting the context
Ensure that the children have been taught the definition of a haiku, tanka and cinquain poem and are aware of how to identify and count syllables in words. Recap if necessary.

Assessment opportunity
Provide each child with the photocopiable pages 'Haiku, tanka and cinquain' and 'Features of poems'. Instruct the children to read each poem, and then to re-read them, tapping out each syllable. Next ask them to underline each syllable with a dash and count the total number of syllables for each line. They should record the syllable count for each line and then identify each poem and record this too. Assess how the children sound out syllables in order to identify the nature of each poem and ask prompt questions such as: *How many syllables has this line got? How many lines are there in the poem? What do you notice about the last line? What impact does the last line or word have? What picture or moment does the poem conjure up?'* There is only a small number of words – *Which sort of words are not included in these poems?* Gather in the completed sheets at the end of the activity.

Assessment evidence
At levels 2–3, children will show some awareness of use of features of organisation, for example, they will be able to identify the first, second and last line of each poem and so on. They will also be able to count the number of syllables in each word. At levels 4–5, children will identify and comment on the features of organisation, for example, the number of lines, numbers of words and number of syllables. They will confidently clap out the syllables and relate this to the poem type. The completed sheet will provide evidence that children are able to analyse a poem in terms of its syllable count and use these features to identify the nature of poems. Use this activity to provide evidence towards Reading AF4.

Next steps
Support: Put children who have difficulty in sounding out syllables to work in groups using percussion instruments to sound out individual words of varying numbers of syllables. Use a text such as *Tanka, Tanka Skunk* by Steve Webb as a stimulus for then reinforcing syllable counts.
Extension: Encourage the children to search through anthologies to find examples of other traditional haikus, tankas and cinquains – tell them to check the syllable count. Explain that some traditional haikus lose their syllable pattern in translation. Can they identify examples where this is the case?

Key aspects of learning
Reasoning: Children will explain their opinions about different poems and use particular words and phrases to support or illustrate their ideas.

Unit 2 Exploring form

Phase ① Features of poems

Learning outcome
Children can understand how the use of expressive and descriptive language can create effects or generate emotional responses.

Success criteria
- I can identify different features in a poem which create an emotional response.
- I can recognise how a poem is performed to create an impact.

Setting the context
Provide pairs of children with the photocopiable page 'Cat poems' (a to d). Allocate different poems to different pairs according to ability. Children working at level 2 could work on *Cats Sleep Anywhere* and those at level 3 could try *Five Little Eyes*. Allocate children at level 4 with *Wanted - A Witch's Cat*, and for children at levels 4-5 *Macavity - The Mystery Cat*. Ask each pair to read their allocated poem, and then to underline the features of the poem such as rhyming couplets, repetition, adjectives, powerful verbs, similes, metaphors and so on. (Write a list on the board if necessary.) Now come back together as a class and read all four poems aloud to the children. Tell them to listen carefully to how the voice is used to create effect.

Assessment opportunity
Following the recital ask children to highlight parts of the poem to demonstrate where the words were spoken loudly, softly, quietly, quickly, fiercely and so on. (Each pair should focus on the particular poem that they studied.) Assess the children's ability to identify features in a poem. Ask children questions to establish their understanding of both the writer's use of language and the meaning of the poem: *Does the poem rhyme? Where do the rhymes occur? Can you show me any interesting phrases? What is the poem about? What image of cats does the poem conjure up in your imagination? How was the poem read to help create this image? Which is your favourite part? Why did you choose this?* At the end of the activity, gather in the annotated sheets. Make a record of the children's oral responses to questioning and their oral responses following the recital of the poems.

Assessment evidence
At levels 2-3, children will comment on what they like or dislike about the poems and they may provide simple reasons for their choices. They may also identify the obvious features in the simple poems, for example, rhyming pairs of words 'anywhere' and 'chair'. They may also make simple statements relating to the effectiveness of language used in the poems such as '"sniffing" is a good word there'. At levels 4-5, children will read and analyse more challenging poems, identify features of the poet's use of language and describe the main purpose, for example, 'It's all about a cat who is a criminal and who cannot be caught'. They may also comment on the impact the poet was hoping to achieve, for example, '"Hidden Paw" is a good way of describing how Macavity is a never there', and the effect the poem had on themselves as readers. The children's annotated poems will provide information against Reading AF6 (see also Reading AF5).

Next steps
Support: Carry out poetry analysis during guided reading sessions. Use open questions to encourage children to express reasons for their likes and dislikes: *Can you find a word/phrase that you really liked? Why did you choose this? What did it make you think of?*
Extension: Have the children study the words to the different poems in *Old Possum's Book of Practical Cats* by TS Eliot. Follow this up by giving them excerpts from *Cats* (the musical) to watch and study how the words have been presented orally. Encourage them to draw the different cats and annotate them with descriptive phrases from the poems which illustrate the cats' personalities.

Key aspects of learning
Self-awareness: Children will discuss and reflect on their personal responses to the texts.
Reasoning: Children will explain their opinions about different poems and use particular words and phrases to support or illustrate their ideas.

Phase ① Reading out loud

Learning outcome
Children can experiment orally with phrases and words to create different effects and responses.

Success criteria
I can perform a poem out loud with expression, change of tone and volume.

Setting the context
After completing the previous activity (poems have been analysed by the children and performed by the teacher and the performance analysed), arrange children into small groups to perform their allocated poems. Ensure that each child has a small part of the poem to perform and experiment with.

Assessment opportunity
As the children read the poems aloud use this as an opportunity to assess their fluency in reading. Assess their ability to use a range of reading strategies effectively when giving their oral presentation. For those children working at levels 2–3, make observations of the strategies adopted to read with fluency and expression. Circulate and observe how children interpret the poem orally within their groups. Comment on use of expression, volume, tone and emphasis. For children working above level 3 for Reading AF1, encourage them to discuss and explain their performance in terms of the poet's intended impact on the listener/reader. You could focus on the assessment of Speaking and listening skills for this group of children.

Assessment evidence
At level 2, children will read a range of key words on sight, for example, 'they', 'don't', 'any' and so on. They will decode unfamiliar words using appropriate strategies such as blending of phonemes and they will read with some fluency and expression, for example, by showing awareness of the exclamation mark at the end of the line, '*They* don't care!'. At level 3, children will use a range of strategies to read with fluency, understanding and expression. Use this activity to gather evidence against Reading AF1.

Next steps
Support: Provide opportunities for children to listen to audio recordings of poetry readings while following the text in order to hear how expression is used to enhance the impact and mood of the poem.
Extension: Provide the opportunity for children to choose a poem to rehearse and perform in front of the class in a recital competition.

Key aspects of learning
Social skills: When designing group presentations, children will learn about relating to the other group members effectively.
Communication: Children will often work collaboratively in pairs and groups. They will communicate outcomes orally, in writing and through ICT.

Phase ② Writing a poem

Learning outcome
Children can write their own haiku poem.

Success criteria
I can write a haiku.

Setting the context
Using the poems about cats that the children have read, alongside images in books or on the internet and the children's own experiences of cats, invite children to fix upon a particular image of a cat. Encourage them to brainstorm words that describe the appearance, nature and behaviour of their chosen cat.

Assessment opportunity
Provide the children with copies of the photocopiable page 'My cat haiku'. Ask the children to draft their haiku, thinking carefully about the words they choose, the order in which they are placed and the syllable count. When the children have completed their first drafts, ask them to pair up and assess each other's poems. Talk partners should give a tick (for a feature they like) and a wish (for something that can be improved). Then ask the children to edit and redraft their poems in light of the comments. Assess children's finished poems in terms of their use of imaginative and interesting ideas: the creation of strong images through the use of similes, metaphors or personification; how the words have been chosen/ordered for effect.

Assessment evidence
At levels 2–3, children will have included mostly relevant ideas in their poems choosing some apt words to create interest. At levels 4–5, children choose relevant ideas and content for their poem with some material developed in detail. The finished poems will provide evidence for Writing AF1 (see also Writing AF3).

Next steps
Support: Provide children with a wordbank to choose from to make up their haiku. Initially children classify the words by syllable count. They can then assemble the words into lines with the correct numbers of syllables.
Extension: Children can attempt to create the same image using cinquain poems. Some children may be able to attempt to draft poems in tanka form.

Key aspects of learning
Evaluation: Children will have regular opportunities to review their work against agreed success criteria. They will view their own and their peers' presentations and discuss ways to improve them.

Phase ② Poetry presentation

Learning outcome
Children can plan, organise and create an ICT-based poetry presentation that involves each member of the group.

Success criteria
I can combine words, images and sounds to create an effective poetry presentation.

Setting the context
Ask the children to work in groups of three to use software such as Windows® Sound Recorder to record their poems, creating effects as appropriate. Tell them to use presentation software such as PowerPoint® to display their text; this may be done using one slide for each line of the haiku or one whole haiku on each slide. Encourage them to use the internet to search for images (copyright permitting) with which to illustrate their recordings. They may choose to manipulate the images to create different effects using photo-editing software. Finally, ask the children to combine the recording with the images and text to produce a poem presentation.

Assessment opportunity
Invite children to share their ideas with you as they are preparing and practising recording their poems, selecting images and word processing their text. How are they going to make their performance effective? What effects will they adopt to create an impact? Gather in the finished presentations at the end of the activity.

Assessment evidence
At levels 2–3, children will sequence and develop their ideas in a simple manner. At levels 4–5, children's development of ideas for their presentation will be organised in a logical sequence. This task provides evidence for Writing AF3.

Next steps
Support: Where children find difficulty in selecting appropriate images to support their poem, clarify the image they are trying to convey by asking questions. Assist

children with keywords to use to search for an appropriate image.
Extension: Children can create presentations of other work using similar techniques, for example, recording extended stories with sound effects and images.

Key aspects of learning
Creative thinking: Children will have the opportunity to respond imaginatively to the stimulus of a first-hand experience and may be able to express their response by presenting poetry through sound and image to enhance its meaning.
Social skills: When designing group presentations, children will learn about relating to the other group members effectively.
Communication: Children will often work collaboratively in pairs and groups. They will communicate outcomes orally, in writing and through ICT.

Phase ③ Evaluating the presentation

Learning outcome
Children can reflect on and evaluate the quality of their peers' poetry presentations.

Success criteria
I can comment constructively on the work of others.

Setting the context
Assign each group a presentation by one of the other groups on which to provide constructive feedback. The children should watch the presentation and discuss the poem, the sound recording, the use of images and the overall effect of the presentation

Assessment opportunity
Give each child a copy of the photocopiable page 'Presentation feedback' and ask them to provide a 'tick and a wish' for each category of assessment. Remind children to be constructive in their comments and to bear in mind the success criteria that were involved at the different stages of the project. (Write these down on the board if it helps.) This peer assessment activity will enable children to give each other valuable feedback and will also provide the opportunity for children to support and learn from each other, thus promoting independent learning.

Assessment evidence
At levels 2–3, children will be able to make simple comments relating to the presentations and they will express likes and dislikes. At levels 4–5, children will be able to give a more detailed critique of the presentation using expressions such as 'I liked the way you... because', 'Your choice of...was very effective because...'. The children's feedback forms will provide evidence for Reading AF6.

Next steps
Support: Model the process of peer assessment for the children. Voice your thoughts while developing your critique of an example presentation so that children develop the necessary language and approach.
Extension: Guide children to develop learning targets from the peer-assessment feedback. How would they move themselves forward in their learning?

Key aspects of learning
Self-awareness: Children will discuss and reflect on their personal responses to the texts.
Reasoning: Children will explain their opinions about different poems and use particular words and phrases to support or illustrate their ideas.
Evaluation: Children will have regular opportunities to review their work against agreed success criteria. They will view their own and their peers' presentations and discuss ways to improve them.

POETRY

Periodic assessment

Reading

Learning outcomes
Children look for and use some technical terms in discussion of poems.
Children can explain how writers have used expressive and figurative language for impact and effect.

Success criteria
● I can recognise a cinquain and explain its features.
● I can recognise a haiku and explain its features.
● I can identify examples of expressive language and explain why the poet has chosen them.

Setting the context
Give each child the photocopiable page 'Poetry 2 Reading assessment', a set of poems about the seasons, and ask them to read it and answer the questions on the sheet. By answering these technical questions about the form of the poems and searching for examples of expressive and figurative language, they can then go on to explain how the poems create an impact on the reader.

Assessment opportunity
Observe the children's ability to identify the structure and organisation of the text. Can they count the syllables on each line? Can they use the number of syllables to identify the type of poem? Assess their ability to identify the purpose of the poem and how the author achieves this. Can they identify expressive language? Can they explain how the author creates an impact?

Assessment evidence
This activity supports the collection of evidence against Reading AF1, AF4 and AF6 and will provide evidence of children's ability to understand the organisation and form of a particular poem and its intended purpose. Use this activity and examples of the children's work throughout this unit to make level judgements regarding their overall progress in Reading.

Writing

Learning outcomes
Children can write a poem about the seasons using a form of their choice.
Children can use ICT to present their poem creatively.

Success criteria
● I can use technical features of a poem to write a haiku, tanka or cinquain.
● I can combine words, images and sound to create a poetic impact.

Setting the context
Children will use the structure of a poetic form to organise and cluster their ideas, using imaginative language to express a viewpoint. They will also use programs such as PowerPoint® or Word® to combine written text with appropriate images and sound effects.

Assessment opportunity
Have children use the photocopiable pages 'Poetry 2 Writing assessment' to stimulate ideas for a poem. Ask them to write their final poem in one of the forms (haiku, tanka or cinquain). Encourage them to develop a multi-media presentation. Assess how well the children develop and organise their ideas.

Assessment evidence
This activity provides evidence against Writing AF1 and AF3. Use this activity and examples of the children's work throughout this unit to make level judgements regarding their progress in Writing.

Haiku, tanka and cinquain

Haiku

- A Japanese form of poem

- Three lines

- Seventeen syllables

- Five syllables on line one

- Seven syllables on line two

- Five syllables on line three

- Usually about nature or the seasons

- Creates a picture from words

Tanka

- A Japanese poem based on the haiku

- It has two extra lines

- It has 31 syllables

- 5, 7, 5, 7, 7 syllable pattern

- Tries to capture the feeling of a moment

Cinquain

- Invented by Adelaide Crapsey

- Total of 22 syllables

- Five lines

- 2, 4, 6, 8, 2 syllable pattern

- Last line is used to add impact or a twist

Name	Date

POETRY

Cat poems (a)

Cats

Cats sleep
Anywhere,
Any table,
Any chair,
Top of piano,
Window-ledge,
In the middle,
On the edge,
Open drawer,
Empty shoe,
Anybody's
Lap will do,
Fitted in a
Cardboard box,
In the cupboard
With your frocks –
Anywhere!
They don't care!
Cats sleep
Anywhere.

Eleanor Farjeon

Use different colours to:

◗ Highlight pairs of rhyming words.

◗ Underline adjectives.

◗ Highlight words that are repeated for effect.

◗ Place a box around your favourite part of the poem and explain why you like it.

Text © 1957, Eleanor Farjeon (1999, Macmillan). Illustration © Bill Houston/Bill Houston Creative Limited.

Red | Amber | Green

○ I can identify different features in a poem which create an emotional response. ▢

○ I can recognise how a poem is performed to create an impact. ▢

Name _____   Date _____

Presentation feedback

This feedback was provided by: _____

This feedback assessed the work of: _____

◾ The poem: (Can you find examples of expressive language? Does the poem follow the format of a haiku?)

✔ _____

⟑ _____

◾ The sound recording: (Has the poem been performed with expression? Have effects been used to enhance the impact of the poem?)

✔ _____

⟑ _____

◾ The images: (Do you think the images chosen enhance the performance? Have the images been presented in a creative way?)

✔ _____

⟑ _____

◾ The overall presentation: (How do the recordings and images fit together to create an overall impact? What would you change to improve the overall impact?)

✔ _____

⟑ _____

Red
Amber
Green   I can comment constructively on the work of others. ☐

◢ Transitional assessment

Activity	Type	Level	Description
2.1	Reading comprehension	2	30-minute two-part test based on a narrative extract from *The Snow Lambs* by Debbie Gliori and the poem 'Weather at Work' by Jenny Morris
2.1	Shorter writing task	2	15 minutes; writing a report about different kinds of weather
2.1	Longer writing task	2	30 minutes; writing a recount based on personal experience of problem weather
3.1	Reading comprehension	3	30-minute two-part test based on narrative extracts from *The Sheep Pig* by Dick King-Smith and a non-fiction leaflet for a farm visitors' centre
3.1	Shorter writing task	3	15 minutes; writing an imaginative description of a special pet
3.1	Longer writing task	3	30 minutes; writing letter to persuade the teacher to take the class on a trip to a farm
4.1	Reading comprehension	4	40-minute two-part test based on extracts from *Street Child* by Berlie Doherty and an historical account about Dr Barnardo
4.1	Shorter writing task	4	20 minutes; writing a report on how a typical day in the classroom has changed since the 19th century
4.1	Longer writing task	4	40 minutes; writing imaginative recounts for Dr Barnardo's diary
5.1	Reading comprehension	5	40-minute two-part test based on non-fiction articles on healthy eating and two poems, 'My brother is making a protest about bread' by Michael Rosen and 'Oh, I wish I'd looked after me teeth' by Pam Ayres
5.1	Shorter writing task	5	20 minutes; writing a leaflet to explain 'Good Health Day'
5.1	Longer writing task	5	40 minutes; writing a cautionary tale about healthy eating

NB There are two transitional assessments provided for each level. Transitional tests and tasks 2.2, 3.2, 4.2 and 5.2 are not shown here. All tests and tasks are available on the CD-ROM.

Reading tests: instructions

There are two reading comprehension tests provided at each level (levels 2–5) on the CD-ROM. Each reading test is divided into two parts.

Administering the test
- Allow 30 minutes for both parts of the test at levels 2 and 3, and 40 minutes at levels 4 and 5.
- Children should work unaided.
- Do not read questions or words to them.

Equipment for each child:
- Pencil, eraser (or children may cross out mistakes).

Marking and levelling the children
- Mark the test using the Reading Mark Scheme provided on CD-ROM.
- Add together the marks from both parts of the reading tests (possible total of 30 marks).
- Use the levelling grid at the end of the Mark Scheme to level the test.
- When awarding an end-of-year Teacher Assessment Level, you will also need to consider a child's performance during Periodic and Day-to-Day Assessments. If a child has achieved a low level 3 or above in the transitional tests, it can be assumed that they have achieved AF1 at that level.

Writing tasks: instructions

There are two writing tasks provided at each level (levels 2–5) on the CD-ROM. Each writing task is divided into two parts: shorter and longer writing tasks.

Administering the tasks

Shorter writing task
Allow 15 minutes for each task at levels 2 and 3, and 20 minutes for each task at levels 4 and 5.

Longer writing task
Allow 30 minutes for each task, which could include 5 minutes' planning time at levels 2 and 3. Allow 40 minutes for each task, which could include 10 minutes' planning time at levels 4 and 5.
- Children should sit so that they cannot see each other's work.
- You may read the task to the children; do not explain the task or help them.
- The task may be administered to groups of children or to the whole class.
- Do not allow children to use dictionaries or word books.

Equipment for each child:
- Pencil, eraser (or children may cross out mistakes) and sheets of plain paper.

Introducing the writing tasks

Say to the children:
I am going to ask you to do some writing.
I will read the task to you, but I cannot help you with your ideas.
If you make a mistake, you should cross it out (or rub it out neatly) and write your word clearly.
Spell the words as best you can, building them up as you usually do.

Marking and levelling the children
- Mark each piece of writing separately using the Writing Mark Scheme, Table 1, provided on the CD-ROM.
- Double the marks gained for the longer Writing task and add this total to the mark gained for the shorter Writing task.
- Assess spelling and handwriting across both pieces of writing using Table 2, provided on the CD-ROM.
- Add the total gained from Table 1 to the total from Table 2.
- Use the grid at the end of the Mark Scheme to find a level for each child.

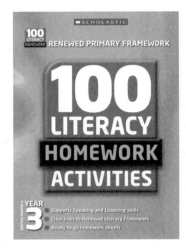